Gay and Sober

Directions for Counseling and Therapy

Gay and Sober

Directions for Counseling and Therapy

Edited by

Thomas O. Ziebold
John E. Mongeon

Gay and Sober: Directions for Counseling and Therapy was originally published in 1982 by The Haworth Press, Inc., under the title *Alcoholism & Homosexuality.* It has also been published as *Journal of Homosexuality,* Volume 7, Number 4, Summer 1982.

Harrington Park Press
New York • Binghamton

ISBN 0-918393-10-8

Published by

Harrington Park Press, Inc.
28 East 22 Street
New York, New York 10010

Harrington Park Press, Inc., is a subsidiary of The Haworth Press, Inc., 28 East 22 Street, New York, New York 10010.

Gay and Sober: Directions for Counseling and Therapy was originally published in 1982 by The Haworth Press, Inc., under the title *Alcoholism & Homosexuality.* It has also been published as *Journal of Homosexuality,* Volume 7, Number 4, Summer 1982.

Library of Congress Cataloging in Publication Data

Alcoholism & homosexuality.
    Gay and sober.

    Previously published as: Alcoholism & homosexuality. c1982.
    Also published as Journal of homosexuality, v. 7, no. 4, summer 1982.
    Includes bibliographies and index.
    1. Homosexuals, Male—United States—Alcohol use—Addresses, essays, lectures. 2. Alcoholism—United States—Addresses, essays, lectures. I. Ziebold, Thomas O. II. Mongeon, John. III. Journal of homosexuality. IV. Title.
HV5139.A43   1985   362.2'92   84-22466
ISBN 0-918393-10-8 (pbk.)

CONTENTS

Foreword   1
John P. De Cecco, PhD

Introduction: Alcoholism and the Homosexual Community   3
Thomas O. Ziebold, PhD
John E. Mongeon

Alcoholism and Homosexuality: A Theoretical Perspective   9
Peter M. Nardi, PhD

Who Should Be Doing What about the Gay Alcoholic?   27
Tricia A. Zigrang, PhD

The Ties that Bind: Strategies for Counseling the Gay Male
Co-Alcoholic   37
Scott Whitney

Counseling the Homosexual Alcoholic   43
Ronnie W. Colcher, MSW

Specific Approaches and Techniques in the Treatment of Gay
Male Alcohol Abusers   53
Tom Mills Smith, MD

A Gay-Identified Alcohol Treatment Program: A Follow-Up Study   71
Rosanne Driscoll, RN, MEd

Alcoholics Anonymous and the Gay Alcoholic   81
   William E. Bittle, PhD

Preventing Alcohol Abuse in the Gay Community: Toward a
 Theory and Model   89
   John E. Mongeon
   Thomas O. Ziebold, PhD

Working Together: The National Association of Gay Alcoholism
 Professionals   101
   Emily B. McNally, MEd, CAC
   Dana G. Finnegan, PhD, CAC

INDEX   105

ABOUT THE EDITORS

Thomas O. Ziebold, PhD, has been active in community alcoholism programs since 1973 as a staff counselor in a residential treatment program, a member of public and private alcoholism councils, a speaker before lay and professional organizations, and a training consultant. As a founder of Washington D.C.'s Gay Counsel on Drinking Behavior, and as Administrator of the Whitman-Walker Clinic, a community-based health care facility for gay men and lesbians, Dr. Ziebold has advocated community attention to the problem of gay alcoholism and drug abuse. He is the author of numerous papers on issues relating to alcoholism and homosexuality and is currently writing a book for counseling gay men.

John E. Mongeon is currently Training Projects Coordinator with University Research Corporation in Washington, D.C., where he authored three training courses in drug abuse prevention for the National Drug Abuse Training Center. He was appointed by the Mayor of Washington, D.C. to represent the gay community on the District of Columbia's Statewide Alcoholism Advisory Council and has served as liaison from the National Association of Gay Alcoholism Professionals to the National Advisory Council of the National Institute on Alcohol Abuse and Alcoholism.

The *Journal of Homosexuality* is devoted to theoretical, empirical, and historical research on homosexuality, heterosexuality, sexual identity, social sex roles, and the sexual relationships of both men and women. It was created to serve the allied disciplinary and professional groups represented by psychology, sociology, history, anthropology, biology, medicine, the humanities, and law. Its purposes are:

    a) to bring together, within one contemporary scholarly journal, theoretical, empirical, and historical research on human sexuality, particularly sexual identity;

    b) to serve as a forum for scholarly research of heuristic value for the understanding of human sexuality, based not only in the more traditional social or biological sciences, but also in literature, history, and philosophy;

    c) to explore the political, social, and moral implications of research on human sexuality for professionals, clinicians, social scientists, and scholars in a wide variety of disciplines and settings.

Gay and Sober

Directions for Counseling and Therapy

FOREWORD

After decades of successful effort to separate homosexuality from its long history of psychiatrization, it is now possible to confront the problem that men and women who are homosexual in desire and practice, like those who are heterosexual, can and do engage in behavior which they may view as injurious to their health and happiness and from which they find it difficult if not impossible to disengage. The ravages of prolonged and excessive drinking have long been portrayed in the daily news about the demise of prominent persons as well as in the novel and theatre, and are the subject of our own observations of friends and coworkers. In the case of homosexuality, individuals seem to add to the social opprobrium for their sexuality a matching self-contempt, the combination of which sends them spinning out of control.

This special issue is a landmark in the gargantuan literature on alcoholism, possibly the first concerted attempt to survey thought on homosexuality and alcoholism and to describe and assess a variety of treatment programs. By necessity the articles cover a broad perspective—theoretical, practical, and exhortatory. For theory, the unflattering psychoanalytic assumptions about homosexuality (in the form of "latent homosexuality") and alcoholism are exposed, and alternative explanations offered. For practice, several approaches to counseling are reviewed, including ways to help the helpers overcome the repugnance they may feel about the homosexuality of their clients. A few of the articles are, I believe, appropriately exhortatory, urging both a greater collective effort in tackling the problem of alcoholism at the national level and, at the local, even personal, level, greater individual responsibility for those who need help.

I wish to thank Thomas Ziebold and John Mongeon for their initial conception of this project and their steadfast, invaluable efforts in bringing it to a successful conclusion. I also express my appreciation to the authors who took time from busy professional schedules to prepare and revise their articles. My thanks also goes to Wendell Ricketts, the new manuscript editor of the *Journal*, for taking over this project with eagerness, energy and consummate editorial skill.

John P. De Cecco, PhD
Editor

INTRODUCTION: ALCOHOLISM
AND THE HOMOSEXUAL COMMUNITY

Thomas O. Ziebold, PhD
John E. Mongeon

Within the last few years the professional literature has begun attending to the needs of homosexual alcoholics. This reflects, or perhaps influenced, the direction in national funding policy initiated by the President's Commission on Mental Health in 1978, which recommended that planning for health services should focus on "at risk" populations and be cognizant of the social and cultural distinctions of the communities served. The President's Commission called attention to homosexual alcoholics as one group that has been inadequately or inappropriately served.

We are pleased to present in this issue of the *Journal of Homosexuality* a collection of papers that summarizes a broad range of individual and program experience in the alcoholism field. Our purpose is to provide a survey of current thought for an audience of gay-oriented and nongay practitioners.

We should state at the outset that this collection of papers is not concerned with the causes of either alcoholism or homosexuality. We do not believe that there is even the slightest evidence of any causal relationship between the two, and to the best of our knowledge, this opinion is shared by all of the authors who have contributed to this issue. Peter Nardi's paper systematically reviews the literature from a theoretical perspective and lays to rest, we believe, many misconceptions and biases in this regard.

Tricia Zigrang reports the clinical experience of a Veterans Hospital, and her paper speaks as much to program and staff development as to client needs and responses. Scott Whitney's paper addresses a different, but wholly related and important concern: the dysfunction of the emotional partner of an alcoholic. Numerous authorities persuade us that alcoholism is a "family" illness, yet they are inevitably speaking in conventional terms of the effects on wife and children of a heterosexual male alcoholic's behavior. Virtually no concern has been directed to the appropriate "family" of a homosexual alcoholic; that is,

Dr. Ziebold is a training consultant in Washington, D.C. His current address is 1659 Hobart Street, NW, Washington, D.C. 20009. Mr. Mongeon is Training Projects Coordinator with University Research Corporation, Washington, D.C.

to the alcoholic's lover and intimate friends who may just as often be suffering the effects of the principal's illness. Scott Whitney's paper is a critical addition to the professional literature, and we only regret that we were not able to solicit more papers on this topic, especially for the lesbian partner.[1]

Ronnie Colcher presents her experience in a suburban private hospital setting which is neither specifically gay-oriented nor closely associated with an urban gay community. Her paper focuses on counseling as opposed to psychotherapy, although it is increasingly difficult in the alcoholism field to differentiate between these disciplines. By contrast, Tom Smith, summarizing the experience of a program in a large general hospital, is located in central San Francisco and encounters a totally different population than Ronnie Colcher in Valley Forge, Pennsylvania. His paper also complements the former with specific therapeutic strategies.

We would like to point out that these two papers exemplify intelligent approaches to a critical issue in alcoholism treatment that extends to all minority groups; namely, the issue of divergence between the social values of therapist (or agency) and client.[2] It is often too easy for therapists and counselors to fall into the erroneous and sometimes damaging stance of believing that their own life-style choices are necessary for the good mental health of other people. This becomes a critical issue in alcoholism treatment where accepted strategies include resocializing, behavior change, and values modification, and where the therapist plays a much more directive role than is perhaps usual in other mental health therapies. Colcher recognizes and indicates the necessary learning process for nongay counselors to understand the diversities between gay and nongay social customs and activities. Equally important, Smith illustrates the need for gay therapists, as well as nongay, to learn about and to work nonjudgmentally with the enormous range of social and sexual values held within the gay subculture.

To complete the various treatment settings, Rosanne Driscoll's paper presents the effectiveness and client outcomes of a gay-oriented, community specific program, and William Bittle discusses Alcoholics Anonymous as it pertains to the needs of homosexual alcoholics in recovery.

We have included our paper on prevention because we think that the gay community is a unique social entity and that its very uniqueness offers a starting point for effective primary prevention campaigns. The final paper in this issue speaks to another aspect of the broader alcoholism field: the support of homosexual women and men who are physicians, therapists, nurses, and counselors.

We have confined this issue to alcoholism and excluded the broader topic

---

[1]The regrettable bias toward the gay male in this issue is due solely to the fact that no papers specific to women's needs were received, despite the editors' best efforts to solicit contributions.

[2]For a further discussion see Ziebold (Note 1).

of drug abuse for several reasons. First, alcoholism affects many more people with much more serious medical consequences than drug addiction. This statement can be substantiated by any number of publications from public and private agencies. Second, most drug abusers in the "gay scene" are also alcohol abusers. We cannot substantiate this statement except by personal observation and hearsay, and we suggest that this is an appropriate topic for intelligent research. Third, alcoholism needs to be addressed as such in a continuing effort to overcome the peculiar public resistance to confronting this major illness.

Alcoholism is a fatal chronic illness affecting the lives of some twenty to thirty percent of the homosexual population as the papers in this issue indicate. This devastating public health problem is, we contend, an epidemic in the technical sense in urban gay communities, calling for intensive prevention efforts by private and public agencies. Yet despite prolonged educational campaigns by many agencies to convince the public of the indisputable medical fact that alcoholism is a chronic illness, albeit of uncertain etiology and symptomatology, our society holds fast to the notion that uncontrollable drinking is degenerate, sinful, or, at the very least, weak-willed—the same bias that society holds against homosexuality. There is adequate evidence that this attitude prevails within the health service professions as well.[3]

The tragic consequence of this stigma is that substantially less than ten percent of the victims of alcoholism seek or receive help for what is, in proven fact, a readily treatable illness. The homosexual alcoholic faces a double stigma that often compounds the denial of adequate health care, as the papers in this collection point out.

The gaybar is a seductive institution. We reckon its place in the minds of most people with the "house of ill repute." Extra-marital fornication has been tolerated in Western culture so long as its practice was primarily confined to the sleazy part of town. Homosexual activities have been tolerated in the same way. Consequently, this establishes the most available milieu in which young people explore being gay: they become exposed primarily to that segment of the homosexual world that is caught up, often compulsively, in the bar scene, and have little opportunity to learn that the gaybar is used by most homosexual people as only a minor adjunct to their social lives.

Merle Miller, in his book *On Being Different* (1971), likens the use of alcohol to wearing a halloween mask that he never wanted to take off. The metaphor is apt. Gay people drink and party to hide from the world, to escape their feelings of being different, and all too many never manage to take off the mask. Shallowness and narcissistic self-indulgence are then interpreted and given public currency as evidence of the "homosexual personality," not as evi-

---

[3]Among the signs of professional bias are efforts to coin euphemisms such as "substance abuser" and "chemically dependent" for the more explicit labels "drunkard," "alcoholic," "junkie," and "addict."

dence of societal confinement. Accepting this view of themselves, the victims accumulate more guilt and more of an urge to escape into drinking. Homosexual adolescents, vulnerably seeking expression of their individuality from family and peers, enter this maelstrom as the only ready outlet for their needs.

Harry Stack Sullivan wrote in the 1940s that:

> With truly distressing frequency, the sundry problems connected with early adolescence cause the person concerned to turn to alcohol, one of the great mental hygiene props in the culture, with unfortunate results. . . . And the problems that get one all too dependent on alcohol are, I think, the problems of sexual adjustment, which hit hardest in early adolescence. (1953, p. 273)

Forty years after he wrote this largely ignored warning, teenage alcoholism is seen as a national crisis.

What can be the effect of continuing to tell adolescents that homosexuality is not acceptable while allowing gay people to gather openly in bars and denying them open entry to our churches? What can be the effect when prominent men and women who are trusted, competent, diligent, and creative remain hidden as homosexuals while the bar-oriented, glitteringly "gay" (i.e., playtime) world is constantly portrayed in the popular press? How can we expect adolescents who happen to be homosexual to escape the enticement towards abusive drinking in a society that remains wholly irrational regarding human sexual expression?

The usual presumption of alcohol treatment programs, implicitly accepted if not explicitly stated, is that if the alcoholic only stops drinking she/he will be returned to the "mainstream of life" as a functioning and useful member of society; generating hope for future happiness lies at the core of therapeutic strategies to combat the morbid despair of alcoholism. What is the American "mainstream" for the homosexual alcoholic in recovery? What hope for eventual serenity do we hold out to the homosexual alcoholic as life's goal?

That most homosexual women and men survive and lead useful lives without contracting alcoholism or drug addiction is testimony to their extraordinary strengths. That most homosexual alcoholics who do seek help recover from their compulsive drinking is further testimony to their extraordinary powers of recuperation and the willing support of those around them. On behalf of that large number who may not escape the illness and on behalf of those adolescents who are now growing up into a society where they will seek to express their differences as homosexuals, we have a particular responsibility to change the social environment both within and outside of the gay world.

We wish to acknowledge the encouragement of the editors and the publisher of the *Journal of Homosexuality* for this special issue. They extend to the professional literature a genuine concern for the well-being of the homosexual community that emerged in the popular gay press in the early 1970s, shortly after the advent of Gay Liberation.[4] Since that time nearly every major gay publication has continued to bring this subject before its community, and we attribute the same motive to novelists such as Larry Kramer and Andrew Holleran who depict the excesses of the gay scene not, we think, vindictively, but out of concern for the growth and wellness of their fellows. We are particularly pleased that the *Journal* has extended this effort to a broader audience.

Above all, we are most indebted to the contributing authors. Without their extracurricular writing effort, for they are all practicing counselors, therapists, or teachers, we would not have had a publication. Our nongay contributors have looked into our community sensitively and our gay contributors have spoken out from within our community candidly. We thank you.

REFERENCE NOTE

1. Ziebold, T. O. Ethical issues in substance abuse treatment relevant to sexual minorities. *Proceedings of the twelfth annual Eagleville conference*, Eagleville, PA: May 1979.

REFERENCES

Jay, K., & Young, A. (Eds.). *After you're out.* New York: Links, 1975.
McGirr, K., & Skinner, R. Alcohol use and abuse in the gay community: A view toward alternatives. *Gay Community News*, May/June 1974.
Miller, M. *On being different.* New York: Random House, 1971.
Sullivan, H. S. *The interpersonal theory of psychiatry.* New York: W. W. Norton, 1953.

---

[4]The earliest article we have seen is McGirr and Skinner, originally published in 1974 and reprinted in Jay and Young (1975, pp. 277–288).

ALCOHOLISM AND HOMOSEXUALITY:
A THEORETICAL PERSPECTIVE

Peter M. Nardi, PhD

ABSTRACT. Although causal relationships between homosexuality and alcoholism have not been established, the myths and assumptions surrounding this issue are numerous. Much of the available literature on the subject is from a psychoanalytic perspective, emphasizing latent homosexuality as a cause of alcoholism. Very little is from the perspective of gay and lesbian populations. This paper analyzes the assumptions underlying the biological and genetic approaches, learning theory, psychoanalytic perspectives, and sociological models as they relate to alcoholism and homosexuality.

Despite some indication of a high estimated rate of alcoholism among homosexuals (Fifield, 1975; Lohrenz, Connolly, Coyne, & Spare, 1978; Saghir & Robins, 1973), relatively little research focuses directly on the subject. This is due in part to the difficulty in delineating a representative sample of homosexual alcoholics. Alcoholism is difficult enough to define, and finding a cross-section of homosexuals (both open gays as well as those still repressed) is unrealistic. It is also due in part to the traditional resistance in social science to studying homosexuality. In either event, the available material is severely limited and of questionable reliability as the following analysis reveals.

The *Journal of Studies on Alcohol* is one of the most important publications in the alcohol field, publishing original articles and abstracts of current alcohol literature. The *Journal's* index serves as an important resource for the field of alcohol studies, with thousands of citations each year. From 1951 through 1980, however, there were only 42 references under the heading of homosexuality.[1]

Dr. Nardi is Associate Professor of Sociology at Pitzer College, Claremont, California. The author wishes to thank Barry Adam, Andrew Berner, Stephen Murray, Farrell Webb, and Thomas Ziebold for their comments and suggestions.

---

[1]Abstracting has not always been as systematic or comprehensive as in recent years. There is, however, no indication that references to homosexuality have been systematically omitted. If errors exist, they probably are randomly distributed throughout the years and across various subtopics. Thus, the numbers in Table 1 should be regarded as not absolute but rather as suggestive of the relative proportion of articles on the subject.

Table 1. Trends in Research on Alcoholism
and Homosexuality Reported in the
Journal of Studies on Alcohol.

Year	Psycho-analytic Studies	Homosexuality as a Demographic	Actual Studies of Gay Men and Lesbians	Total
1951-1960	12 (a)	5	2 (b)	19
1961-1970	0	5	1 (c)	6
1971-1980	0	7	10	17
	---	---	---	---
	12	17	13	42

Notes:
  (a) Three of these were not supportive of the psycho-analytic model.
  (b) Both used gays as a control group only.
  (c) A case study of an alcoholic with homosexual tendencies.

As shown in Table 1, only 10 of those references (24% of the total 42) were actual studies of alcohol use among homosexuals. The remainder were either (1) references to latent homosexuality and its undocumented causal relationship to alcoholism (29%), (2) studies using homosexuality as one of several pieces of demographic data, but not focusing on it (40%), or (3) research using homosexuals as a control group to compare with alcoholics, under a psycho-analytic research model (7%). In short, less than one tenth of one percent of all available references in 30 years are on alcohol use among homosexuals, despite high estimates of alcoholism and much anecdotal concern over homosexual drinking patterns.

The relationship between alcoholism and homosexuality has had an unusual history. For decades, followers of Freudian thought have sought to explain alcoholism simply in terms of latent homosexuality. Today, more complex sociocultural theories are often offered to describe the relationship between problem drinking and homosexuality. Somewhere between the early psychoanalytic ideas and the current sociocultural views is a vast chasm of misguided research, theories, and unanswered questions. Although causal relationships have not been established, the myths and assumptions that surround this issue are numerous. This paper is a beginning step in organizing what is known about the relationship between alcoholism and homosexuality. It is an analysis and exploration of underlying assumptions, focusing on several theoretical perspectives and concluding with suggestions for much needed further investigation using a sociological approach.

No attempt is made in this paper to define alcoholism specifically. Rather, the focus is on drinking patterns in general, with particular emphasis on problem drinking or alcoholism. The words "gay" and "lesbian" refer to those men and women who are open about their homosexual identity either to themselves or to others, although "gay" will be used for brevity to include both men and women. "Repressed homosexuals" are those who have not accepted their sexual identity.

The current trend, however, is clearly in the direction of research on homosexual populations and away from a psychoanalytic model. This is illustrated by the recent appearance of articles on alcoholism in gay magazines and newspapers (such as Abramson, 1979; Anderson, 1979 and Shilts, 1976 in the *Advocate*; Bowring, 1979 in *Gay Community News*; Ziebold, 1979 in *Christopher Street*), by special sessions of professional meetings (such as the 1980 National Council on Alcoholism in Seattle), by the formation of the National Association of Gay Alcoholism Professionals, and by the publication of gay-oriented materials by several alcohol agencies (such as Michael, 1976 & 1977 for CompCare; Schwartz, 1980 for *Do It Now Foundation*; Alcoholics Anonymous, Alcoholism Center for Women in Los Angeles, Hazelden Educational Services, and Wisconsin Clearinghouse for Alcohol and Other Drug Information). This trend coincides with major social and intellectual advances with respect to homosexuality issues between 1950 and 1980. However, many of the recent scholarly publications on alcoholism and homosexuality are anecdotal or contain serious methodological problems. In fact, the figures usually introduced to support excessive alcoholism rates among homosexuals come from studies with limited generalizability.

The most quoted figure is from Fifield's (1975) study conducted for Los Angeles County by the Gay Community Services Center. Gathering self-report data from 200 gay bar users, 98 bartenders and owners, 53 recovered gay alcoholics in treatment programs, and 132 users of the Services Center, Fifield estimates problem drinking rates in the gay population as three times higher than rates in the general population. Based on bartenders' estimates, Fifield concludes that 10.4% of the total adult gay population in Los Angeles County are a "primary target group of gay men and women in crisis or danger stages of alcohol consumption and in need of alcoholism services" (p. 8). A secondary target group in high risk of needed future treatment is estimated as 21% of the gay population. Thus, 31.4% of the Los Angeles County gay and lesbian population show signs of alcoholism or heavy drinking. Given the dependency on bar goers and bartenders, the use of self-reported problem drinking, the lack of a control group of heterosexual bar goers, and the derivation of figures from previously estimated percentages, this study has limited generalizability and reliability.

Another highly quoted finding comes from a study of 145 homosexual men selected from two Kansas university towns and two Kansas cities (Lohrenz et al., 1978). Most of the subjects were college educated, were current students or professionals, and were from urban areas. Based on scores on the Michigan Alcoholism Screening Test (MAST), 29% of the homosexual sample were categorized as alcoholic. The failure to obtain a control group, to verify the MAST scores with more detailed questions, and to survey a more representative cross-section of gay people also limits the reliability and validity of these findings.

Saghir and Robins (1973) included a few questions on drinking behavior in their three to four hour long interviews with 89 male and 57 female homosexuals. Their sample was selected mostly from gay political/social organizations (about 65%), through word-of-mouth (about 25%), and from gay bars (between 5 and 10%) in Chicago and San Francisco. Among lesbians, 35% described their drinking behavior as excessive or alcohol dependent at some point in their lives. Among a control group of 43 heterosexual women, 5% described their drinking as excessive or dependent at some point in their lives.

Among gay men, 30% said they were excessive or dependent drinkers at some point in their lives. Among a control group of 35 heterosexual men, 20% described their drinking as excessive or alcohol dependent at some point in their lives. Problems with the study are its small sample size, its limited representativeness of the gay population, and its dependence on only a few questions about drinking behavior.

Besides these studies, no other research has been published with statistical data on drinking rates among gay and lesbian populations. Weinberg and Williams (1974) in their survey of over 2000 gay men included *one* question on drinking in their 145-question survey ("Do you ever drink more than you should?" never/hardly ever/sometimes/many times). The poor and biased phrasing of that question; the dependence on Mattachine members and gay bar users in New York, San Francisco, Amsterdam, and Copenhagen; and the low response rate (averaging about 30%) severely limit the reliability of the finding (27.9% responded sometimes and 11.4% said many times).

The highly publicized Bell and Weinberg (1978) "Kinsey study" of almost 1000 San Francisco homosexuals failed to include a single question on drinking behavior. Even Read's (1980) ethnography of a male gay bar did not include any detailed descriptions or discussions of drinking styles, attitudes, or patterns.

Several descriptive articles on gay alcoholics have recently appeared oriented toward the counseling profession. Small and Leach (1977) discuss case histories of 10 gay male alcoholics and offer suggestions for counseling; Diamond and Wilsnack (1978) report descriptive findings from 10 lesbian alcohol abusers, revealing strong dependency needs, low self-esteem, and depression among their clients; and Beaton and Guild (1976) describe their group counseling sessions with three gay men and two lesbians and offer strategies for nongay therapists.

Other published articles on the topic include a survey of nongay alcoholism treatment agencies and the services offered for gay men and women (Judd, 1978), a discussion of lesbianism and alcoholism (Hawkins, 1976), and an interview with a lesbian alcoholic (Sandmaier, 1979).

In sum, the direction of research in recent years is toward understanding alcohol use from within the gay community. However, the current literature on homosexuality and alcoholism does not yet include a systematic, rigorous epidemiological survey of alcoholism or of drinking patterns among the gay subculture. The attention that is growing and the interest in the topic that is developing are positive signs for future quality research. Understanding the assumptions underlying prior research on the subject and sharpening the conceptual frameworks for new research are important first steps in achieving the quality that is much needed in this area.

Theoretical Perspectives

The shift from the historical dominance of the psychoanalytic model to the current trend in studying gay alcoholics from a sociocultural perspective, represents not only a major change in society's knowledge about and attitude toward homosexuality, but also a shift in theoretical perspectives and assumptions about alcoholism. An analysis of each of the major theoretical viewpoints and how it may relate to homosexuality will clarify the myths and assumptions many people hold about the connection between alcoholism and homosexuality and will enhance the ability to evaluate past research and to set the foundation for quality research. Several theoretical viewpoints exist concerning the etiology of alcoholism: biological-genetic, psychoanalytic, learning, and sociocultural (see Buss, 1966).

Biological-Genetic Arguments

Some have viewed alcoholism as a function of anatomy, physiology, metabolic abnormalities, tissue chemistry, allergies, enzyme defects, or genetic transmission (see Kessel & Walton, 1965). One of the major studies supporting a genetic model is Goodwin's (1976) work with Danish children. He demonstrated that male offspring of alcoholics, separated from their biological parents in early infancy and raised by nonrelatives, had "nearly twice the number of alcohol problems and four times the rate of alcoholism as the children whose parents had no record of hospitalization for alcoholism" (p. 73). This suggested to Goodwin a genetic predisposition to severe alcohol abuse. Goodwin (1979) has also argued that what is inherited is not a predisposition to alcohol, but a lack of intolerance for alcohol. Those with the allergy to alcohol are the ones who avoid it and remain nonalcoholic.

These studies tend to locate the etiology of alcoholism in biological or genetic abnormalities. Deficiencies or pathologies in the physiological system affect reactions and responses to alcohol. Although biological or genetic explanations cannot be ruled out entirely, no conclusive evidence has yet been presented to establish a dominant biological or genetic trait for alcoholism.

Similarly, some have presented biological or genetic abnormalities to explain homosexuality, usually emphasizing hormonal imbalances (Glass, Deuel, & Wright, 1940; Lang, 1940) or heredity (Kallman, 1952). Wilson (1978), from a sociobiological position, even discusses a genetic predisposition to be homosexual. However, no substantial evidence has been forthcoming to support these early studies in establishing a dominant biological or genetic basis for homosexuality (see West, 1967).

Although no one has made the connection explicit or published research on the subject, some dedicated biologically oriented theorists could easily attempt to search for biological or genetic variables to explain both homosexuality and alcoholism simultaneously. Perhaps, they might argue, the reason for high incidences of drinking problems among homosexuals is some shared gene or hormonal imbalance. More importantly, the assumptions underlying a nature-oriented form of inquiry involve a "what-went-wrong" philosophy; that is, deviations from "normal" or "natural" genetic/biological structures are used to describe why the individual ended up both homosexual and alcoholic. By locating the source of behavior in biological or genetic factors, oppressive social conditions are absolved or overlooked.

While genetic or biological theories might combine with other theories in explaining the issue and, thus, contribute to our understanding of alcoholism among homosexuals, the potential misuse of them as *sole* explanations could prove more detrimental to our understanding of behavior.

Psychoanalytic Tradition

Nowhere is the relationship between alcoholism and homosexuality more distorted than in psychoanalytic theories. As was demonstrated in Table 1, most of the published material cited in 30 years of the *Journal of Studies on Alcohol* abstracts, especially during the 1950s, derives from a psychoanalytic perspective and emphasizes a causal relationship between latent homosexuality and alcoholism. In fact, the link between the two has been explicitly made since the early 1900s. As Buss (1966) states: "Classical psychoanalytic theory emphasizes orality and homosexuality in the genesis of alcoholism" (p. 445).

Alcoholics are seen to be fixated in either the oral or anal stage, to over-identify with the father, to be anxious about masculine inadequacy and incompleteness, to have emotionally absent fathers and overindulgent mothers, to have experienced traumatic weaning, to exhibit penis envy, or to have an irrational fear of being heterosexual (Buss, 1966; Roebuck & Kessler, 1972; Small & Leach, 1977). These same phrases are often used by psychiatrists to describe the etiology of homosexuality (see Bieber, Dain, Dince, Drellich, Grand, Gundlach, Kremer, Rifkin, Wilbur, & Bieber, 1962; Socarides, 1968).

Modern psychoanalytic theory less often insists that homosexuality is basic to alcoholism, emphasizing more that homosexual urges are controlled by drinking behavior. Yet, erroneous assumptions and myths about homosexuality persist. For example, Hatterer (1970) responds as follows to a client troubled by his homosexual experiences: "You're right about your homosexual activities being directly triggered by your drinking. I'd go so far to say now it's possible you'd stop all of it if you were sober" (p. 249). Levy (1958) also draws on faulty reasoning when he writes:

> Transient overt homosexual contacts while drinking . . . are not uncommon among patients. In most cases this represents the lack of concern with, and clear perception of, the nature and needs of the sexual object. In most cases a woman or a sheep might have done as well. (p. 656)

Similar sexist assumptions have guided research conducted with homosexuals as control groups. Rather than studying alcoholism among homosexual populations, researchers have tended to look for homosexuality (as defined by masculinity-femininity scales) among alcoholics. A 1959 study by Machover, Puzzo, Machover, & Plumeau, using M-F scales and projective tests, confirmed a hypothesis that remitted alcoholics would exhibit more homosexual tendencies than unremitted alcoholics. They based this hypothesis on "the clinical impression that tendencies toward feminine, including maternal, identification were more frequent among the remitted alcoholics" (p. 529).

Gibbons and Walters (1960) also assumed a psychoanalytic model to test the relationship between latent homosexuality and alcoholism, using a control group of "self-confessed manifest homosexuals" who had been "arrested for homosexual offenses." They reason that

> If there is any substance to the belief that alcoholic males are latent homosexuals, one might expect that they and nonalcoholic manifest homosexuals would perceive certain stimuli in their environment in a somewhat similar manner, i.e., that in some respects alcoholics would differ from normal subjects and resemble homosexuals. (p. 618)

However, their findings were mixed, failing to show any differences between subjects in one experiment and, in two other experiments, showing alcoholics as scoring between homosexuals and "normals." Yet, Gibbins and Walters conclude: "While the experiments as a whole do not provide strong evidence for the psychoanalytic theory, the results suggest that this theory should not be lightly discarded" (p. 618). Interpreting results to conform to firmly held assumptions is also evident in one of Tahka's (1966) conclusions from his study of 50 male alcoholics in Stockholm: "All the subjects preferred men to women as drinking companions. This might be interpreted as an indication of latent homosexual needs" (p. 179).

The relationship between latent homosexuality and alcoholism is even expressed in artistic form in Tennessee Williams' 1955 play *Cat on a Hot Tin Roof*. Brick's alcoholism is linked to his frustrating relationship with his wife Maggie and his repressed homosexual feelings about his dead friend Skipper. Lolli (1956) sees in this play an illustration of the psychoanalytic refrain: "Oral frustrations contribute both to alcoholism and homosexuality. Therefore, the presence of latent homosexual traits in alcoholics is neither unusual nor mild" (p. 550).

Critics of this perspective attack the overemphasis on oral aspects of homosexuality. The typical psychoanalytic approach usually ignores the range of sexual practices and the emotional-love dimensions of same-sex relationships. Furthermore, it does not account for lesbians, for the repressed homosexuals who are not alcoholic, for the open gays and lesbians who are not alcoholic, and for the open gays who are alcoholic (Small & Leach, 1977). While repression of fundamental characteristics of self can often lead to destructive behavior, the focus of psychoanalysis is of particular relevance here. The relationship between latent homosexuality and alcoholism assumes that learning to overcome one's repressed homosexual feelings and to live heterosexually is the best "cure" for alcoholism. Thus, the focus of therapy is on one's sexuality, not on the drinking or the repression. In other words, when a pathology is linked to repressed homosexuality in psychiatry, the link is made to the homosexuality instead of to the repression (Adam, 1978). Szasz (1970) similarly has criticized psychiatry for manufacturing mental illness and labeling homosexuality as a disease, thereby obscuring the fact that homosexuals are medically stigmatized and socially persecuted.

Connecting a disease concept of homosexuality with a disease concept of alcoholism, however, makes sense from a psychoanalytic therapeutic viewpoint (see Conrad & Schneider, 1980). Each disease can then be cured with similar techniques, psychoanalysis or aversion therapy, and only by medical experts. Adam (1978) has described the historical role of therapeutic ideologies in perpetuating inferiorization and domination among gay people. The psychoanalytic model has served to maintain internalization of negative self-images. As Adam states:

> The psychiatric literature provides a compendium of the responses to domination; it is a vast document of the contempt internalized by an inferiorized people from a society which stands opposed to its self-realization. The "cure" is the disease. Acting as an agent of inferiorization,

the therapeutic establishment cannot but compound the malaise of the oppressed. (pp. 41-2)

In short, psychoanalytic theory has been the major source of false assumptions concerning the relationship between alcoholism and homosexuality. Psychoanalytic research on alcoholism and psychoanalytic treatment of alcoholics exhibiting homosexual behavior, as a result, have suffered from the use of oppressive and sexist concepts and methodologies.

Learning Theory

If psychoanalytic theory focuses on inner thought and feelings, a learning approach emphasizes more overt behavior. From this perspective, alcoholism is seen as a learned behavior resulting from reinforcement of pleasurable experiences or from avoidance of negative ones. Tension reduction, relaxation, peer approval, and feelings of power have all been listed as associated with drinking alcohol (Schuckit & Haglund, 1977).

Akers (1973) believes that drinking patterns are a "function of the social rewards attached to drinking and the reinforcing effects of the alcohol" (p. 127). Negative reinforcement occurs when anxiety is reduced and stressful situations are avoided. Positive reinforcement occurs when social groups reward drinking behavior and when pleasurable effects are experienced. When negative sanctions are applied to what begins to seem like excessive drinking, these punishing sanctions become weak, irregular, and infrequent compared with the numerous rewards of drinking behavior (Trice, 1966). Imitation of peers' and elders' drinking patterns is also viewed as a dominant characteristic of initial learning experiences with alcohol (Maddox, 1962).

Thus, learning theorists view social sanctions and norms concerning drinking behavior as important components in explaining drinking patterns and alcoholism. Since learning theorists posit reinforcement schedules, some also believe that unlearning behavior can occur through similar means. Aversion techniques, ranging from nausea-inducing drugs, such as Antabuse, to electric shock treatment, are often prescribed for alcohol dependent people (Steffen, Steffen, & Nathan, 1977).

Similar reinforcement arguments have been offered to explain homosexual behavior as learned behavior. Some believe it also can be unlearned. The misguided use of electric shock therapy to unlearn homosexuality and reinforce heterosexuality is well documented (see Adam, 1978). Others see homosexual behavior as a gradual process of reinforcement and rationalization (Akers, 1973). Inhibitions toward homosexuality decrease as positive rewards accrue from direct homosexual experiences, from masturbatory imagery, and relatively less positive heterosexual experiences (Akers, 1973). As participation in a gay subculture increases, often at first through bars, emerging gay people develop rationalizations and justifications for their behavior. Social rewards and minimization of anxiety over being different increase, thus leading to the continuation of homosexual behavior (Akers, 1973).

A learning model explanation of excessive drinking among gays and lesbians stresses tension-reduction and the more positive hedonistic aspects of the open and visible gay community. For some gay people just coming out, getting involved sexually with another of the same biological sex is possible only while intoxicated (Chafetz, Blane, & Hill, 1970). The tension, anxiety, and guilt feelings generated in the context of a society which does not condone homosexual behavior are reduced by increased alcohol use. The resultant strength and feelings of power allow emerging gay people to make sexual contacts and overcome social resistances.

Another possible explanation is the positive reinforcements of an open gay life-style which stresses bar life and drinking. The emergence of gay bars as a common institution for introduction into a gay community derives from their history of permissiveness and protectiveness (Achilles, 1967). Gay bars emphasize the leisure time dimensions of one's gay identity; they provide some anonymity and segregation from the dominant culture and permit sexual contacts to be made with relative safety and respectability (Achilles, 1967). Hooker (1965) has also described gay bars as centers for communication among the gay community and as free markets retailing both leisure time activities, such as entertainment and drinking, and sexual services. That gay bars serve a wide range of needs, interests, and goals in often highly ritualized ways is documented in Read's (1980) ethnography of a working-class gay male bar. Whatever the motives of gay bar patrons, and whatever needs are being filled, the importance and availability of alcohol in achieving their goals is strongly evident in the gay bar subculture.

Other social activities within the gay community, as well as the gay media, constantly encourage a fashionable social scene replete with alcohol (Warren, 1974). This mirrors the dominant culture's emphasis on drinking as an acceptable component of a successful social event. As Warren states: "There is pressure to drink alcohol. . . . Getting drunk in gay bars, like getting drunk at home gatherings, is normal trouble in the gay community, rather than deviance" (p. 58).

This might explain why some open gays and lesbians drink heavily, not because of anxiety or low self-esteem, but because of the acquired habit of drinking in gay settings. The positive aspects of being a part of a gay community reinforce drinking patterns. Drinking is not used to escape from something; rather it is used to join something. Initial socialization into a gay community often occurs by attending gay bars and by enacting the drinking roles perceived as essential for a gay identity. Whether heavy drinking may be for some the outcome of continually reinforced positive feelings engendered by the gay life-style and not due to negative feelings has yet to be systematically explored.

As with all subcultures, there exists a diversity of people within the group. There are many different types of homosexuals; there are many different types of alcoholics and alcoholisms. Searching for a single etiology to explain all drinking by homosexuals or to explain all forms of alcoholism is a misguided task. For some open gays, a pleasure-seeking explanation is probably a more accurate learning model. For others just "coming out," a tension-reduction model may serve as a sharper explanation, especially in the context of emerging positive rewards as contact is made with a gay community. For those still "in the closet" and repressing their identity, a tension-reduction model may also be an appropriate framework for understanding their drinking behavior. Thus, learning theory can offer several avenues of research for analyzing drinking behavior patterns among various types of gay people at various stages of identity formation.

A Sociocultural Approach

Variations in rates of alcoholism from one society to another, and from one subculture to another, have led many to seek a sociocultural explanation for drinking patterns and behaviors. Kessel and Walton (1965) emphasize such factors as incitement (money, leisure time, advertising), opportunity (social class, occupation, number of area bars, laws), and example (peers and parents) as contributors to alcohol use and abuse. Trice (1966) has focused on the social values, rules, and meanings a particular group gives to alcohol, and Bales (1946) has offered a model of three interacting sets of factors: dynamic factors, alternative factors, and orienting factors. Dynamic factors include acute psychic tensions at the group level; alternative factors are culturally defined patterns of behavior other than heavy drinking but functionally equivalent in relieving acute psychic tensions; and orienting factors involve the group's traditional ways of defining the norms and attitudes about drinking.

Some have developed anomie theories for explaining the source of tension and anxiety experienced by the incipient alcoholic. Snyder (1964) emphasizes the low rate of alcoholism among culturally integrated and cohesive societies and the higher rate among societies with more social disorganization. Ullman (1958) similarly stresses the importance of inconsistent drinking norms and unintegrated drinking customs in producing ambivalent feelings about drinking. Room (1976), on the other hand, rejects the concept of ambivalence as an explanation for problematic drinking behavior.

Others have argued that drinking behavior is related to definitions emerging out of social interaction, emphasizing the power of labels and socially constructed meanings within a culture. MacAndrew and Edgerton (1969), for example, refute the universality of the disinhibiting effects of alcohol. They observed, in numerous cross-cultural settings, that social behavior while drunk is highly variable and situationally defined. How a society defines drinking and drunkenness, what meanings are constructed for behavior "under the influence," and what situational factors and social norms are relevant, all affect drinking patterns and definitions of alcoholism.

Furthermore, some argue that definitions of drinking problems and behaviors are imposed by those in power to make and enforce rules (Conrad & Schneider, 1980). The emergence of the temperance movement as a crusade symbolic of the power of the ruling class illustrates the process of socially defining, transmitting, labeling, and controlling drinking behavior (Gusfield, 1963). Duster (1970) also describes the relationship among social class, power, and definitions of substance abuse as immoral or illegal.

Changing social structural conditions also have been demonstrated to affect drinking behavior. Brenner (1973) shows that "psychiatric hospitalization of persons diagnosed as having psychosis with alcoholism increases sharply during economic downturns and decreases during upturns" (p. 225).

In short, a sociocultural view of alcohol use emphasizes the norms and values of the society toward drinking, the meanings people attach to drinking, and the definitions and laws imposed by those in power to enact and control the norms.

Similarly, one can develop a sociocultural analysis of homosexuality, focusing on a society's definitions, norms, and attitudes toward it. By viewing the social context in which an individual is socialized (for example, social class, ethnic background, religious influences, family dynamics), a clearer understanding can emerge of how a person acquires a sexual identity and what is done with it by society and by the individual. Instead of defining homosexuality as an illness or pathology, therefore, a sociocultural perspective emphasizes the meanings given by people and by those in power to homosexual behavior. Stigma, oppression, individual rage and anxiety are seen to be created by the social context and cannot be fully understood apart from the dominant culture's values and beliefs (Hills, 1980). The fact that homosexuality has been variously regarded through time as a sin, a sickness, a moral issue, a legal issue, and a life-style illustrates the importance of social definitions in how gay people are treated and how they perceive themselves (Conrad & Schneider, 1980).

An analysis of drinking behavior within gay and lesbian subcultures, then, employing a sociocultural model, leads to a more complex and less reductionistic understanding of the issue. Unless the problem is viewed from the perspective and social context of gay people, inappropriate research methodologies and misguided assumptions will persist. As Robinson (1976) states in his call for a sociological study of alcoholism:

> . . . we must not take for granted at the outset what "alcoholism," or "drinking problem", or "being an alcoholic" is. What is needed instead is

an understanding of what these things mean to particular people in particular situations. (p. 8)

If one focuses on the social context in which gay people find themselves, how they define reality and perceive their situation, and what symbols and values they hold with respect to alcohol use, a more complete picture of the relationship between homosexuality and alcoholism begins to develop.

Emphasizing the point that gay people congregate in bars is too simple an explanation for understanding their drinking patterns. It is only one factor ("opportunity" in Trice's perspective, or "orienting factors" in Bales') among many which interact. A necessary starting point in understanding homosexual drinking patterns is to focus on

> the inner world of alcoholism—with the view from inside out rather than outside in. . . . We must, in effect, put aside our own frame of reference and be willing to enter into that of another to see how he makes sense of his experiences and reacts to them. (Wallace, 1977, p. 6)

Understanding how certain gay individuals manage and control their feelings in an oppressive social context illustrates this phenomenological perspective. A homophobic society instills in those coming to terms with their sexuality a variety of feelings about the immorality and deviant nature of homosexuality. A typical response is to deny to oneself (and often loudly to others) that one is homosexual. Self-hatred, fear of being different, and lowered self-esteem often lead to strong ego defenses and rigid denial (Ziebold, 1978). Hiding one's feelings, sexual and otherwise, becomes normative. Thus, homosexuals trying to "come out" find they must struggle not only against society's expectations, but also against their own perceptions. Some may give up, becoming alienated from their own feelings. They hide behind the closet door, locked securely by the illusion of safety while slowly destroying their own identity and mental health.

These dynamic factors may also lead some to increase their consumption of alcohol to aid in their "coming out" process or to maintain their concealed identity. As Ziebold (1979) writes, "Homosexual individuals who have been forced to develop rigid defenses against social reaction to their sexual and affectional orientation may unknowingly let these same reflexes reinforce a budding dependency on alcohol" (p. 39). Given the orienting factors of socially approved drinking settings, such as parties and gay bars, alcohol can easily become, for those coming out, one means of coping with the perceived oppressive social situation and personal psychic confusion. The absence of significant, subculturally valued alternatives to drinking settings, especially in the smaller, less urban centers, contributes to the dependency on alcohol as an acceptable solution to feelings of anxiety, alienation, and low self-esteem. This, of course, is not much different from the role of alcohol in heterosexual society, except that for many heterosexuals, there are numerous socially sanctioned, positive alternative sources of dependency. Social interaction does not always depend on singles' bars; family bonds may often be stronger, and work-related friendships may be closer. For those heterosexuals who also find these factors absent, vulnerability to the alcohol alternative increases. Although the absence of these factors can often be replaced by newer social ties to gay groups and "families" (Nardi, in press), the gay person just "coming out" or the repressed homosexual would probably not as yet have made these new connections. For some open gays for whom the absence of these factors may be acute, for those homosexuals not yet involved in a gay subculture (still "in the closet"), and for those still repressing their identity, alcohol can easily become a source of dependency and strength. Ziebold (1979) clearly illustrates this sociocultural model when he writes:

> A high level of psychic stress, polarization towards bars and cocktail parties as the primary basis for social interaction, and a closing off of alternative modes of relief in everyday living: these are the forces of oppression, and alcoholism is one of the resulting symptoms. (p. 40)

The dilemma faced by gay and lesbian alcoholics is further heightened when one considers the additional stigma of alcoholism. Concealing from oneself and from others that one is an alcoholic is a common practice. Whether this is a function of an unconscious denial process, is due to a society imposing negative labels on certain forms of drinking behavior, or is a result of epistemological confusion [i.e., difficulty in coming to know oneself due to conflicting labels, social comparisons, and mixed outcomes with alcohol use (Wallace, 1977)], there is clearly an attempt to hide oneself behind another closed door. Alcoholism has historically been treated as a crime, a sin, a moral issue, a legal matter, or, more recently, a disease (Conrad & Schneider, 1980). But even today, it is kept quiet in families, concealed at work, and hidden from others. Being labeled alcoholic has been as stigmatizing as being labeled homosexual (see Goffman, 1963).

Confined by double closet doors, gay and lesbian alcoholics must work on opening both. As alcoholics, homosexuals must hide their drinking from other gays for fear of rejection; as homosexuals, alcoholics must hide their sexuality from heterosexual alcoholics or therapists for fear of rejection (Ziebold, 1979). The problems are further intensified if the gay alcoholic is a member of another minority also oppressed and stigmatized by society. Women, blacks, Hispanics, and Native Americans are some of those who face additional blocks to finding positive alternative sources of identity and support. Alienation, low self-esteem, and morally weak labels are maintained by the social system, thereby increasing vulnerability to addictive behavior. How society defines and regulates interactions and roles for homosexuals, alcoholics, and other minorities must be analyzed first. Studying how these people define their situation and attempt to express their feelings in this social context will lead to a fuller understanding of the complex, dynamic relationship between homosexuality and alcoholism.

Summary

As with any social phenomenon, adopting a particular theoretical framework structures the kinds of questions asked and limits the range of answers offered. A biological or genetic perspective tends to focus on deviations from what is assumed to be natural. Anomalies, illnesses, and pathologies are described, and variations in "normal" behavior become so labeled. Overlooked or de-emphasized are the social structural factors and environmental strains which may be contributing to the "deviant" behavior.

Psychoanalytic paradigms focus attention on latent homosexuality, thereby failing to account for problem drinking among open gays and lesbians. Further-more, assumptions underlying this perspective emphasize the "deviant" sex-uality and not the societal conditions leading to the repression.

Learning theory models best contribute to our understanding of why some of those openly gay and involved in a gay subculture may become alcoholic. Socialization into a hedonistic, positively reinforcing life-style revolving around bars and other alcohol-oriented social functions is offered as an explanation by this perspective. Future research needs to focus more on the positive di-mensions many perceive while learning to become a member of a gay subcul-ture of bars and parties.

A more encompassing viewpoint is the sociocultural one, emphasizing label-ing theories, conflict models, and interactionist perspectives. Understanding drinking behavior and patterns among gay populations necessitates analysis of the meanings and definitions of alcohol use people within a subculture evolve. How those in power structure the roles of gay people and alcoholics, how they define problem drinking and alcoholism, and how gay people in turn respond to these structures and definitions are the issues this perspective emphasizes.

By clarifying models for research and assumptions underlying various theo-retical perspectives, our understanding of the relationship between homosex-uality and alcoholism will be enhanced and our strategies for prevention and treatment can only improve.

REFERENCES

Abramson, M. Loving an alcoholic. *Christopher Street*, August 1979, pp. 15-17.
Achilles, N. The development of the homosexual bar as an institution. In J. Gagnon & W. Simon (Eds.), *Sexual deviance*. New York: Harper and Row, 1967.
Adam, B. *The survival of domination*. New York: Elsevier, 1978.
Akers, R. *Deviant behavior: A social learning approach*. Belmont, CA: Wadsworth Publishing, 1973.

Anderson, S. Beating the bottle the gay way. *Advocate*, June 28, 1979, pp. 25;27.

Bales, R. Cultural differences in rates of alcoholism. *Quarterly Journal of Studies on Alcohol*, 1946, *6*, 480-499.

Beaton, S., & Guild, N. Treatment for gay problem drinkers. *Social Casework*, 1976, *57*(5), 302-308.

Bell, A., & Weinberg, M. *Homosexualities: A study of diversity among men and women*. New York: Simon and Schuster, 1978.

Bieber, I., Dain, H., Dince, P., Drellich, M., Grand, H., Gundlach, R., Kremer, M., Rifkin, A., Wilbur, C., & Bieber, T. *Homosexuality: A psychoanalytic study*. New York: Basic Books, 1962.

Bowring, D. HATS helps gay alcoholics. *Gay Community News*, December 8, 1979, pp. 10-12.

Brenner, M. H. *Mental illness and the economy*. Cambridge: Harvard University Press, 1973.

Buss, A. *Psychopathology*. New York: John Wiley, 1966.

Chafetz, M., Blane, H., & Hill, M. *Frontiers of alcoholism*. New York: Science House, 1970.

Conrad, P., & Schneider, J. *Deviance and medicalization: From badness to sickness*. St. Louis: Mosby, 1980.

Diamond, D., & Wilsnack, S. Alcohol abuse among lesbians: A descriptive study. *Journal of Homosexuality*, 1978, *4*(2), 123-142.

Duster, T. *The legislation of morality: Law, drugs, and moral judgment*. New York: Free Press, 1970.

Fifield, L. *On my way to nowhere: Alienated, isolated, drunk*. Los Angeles: Gay Community Services Center and Department of Health Services, 1975.

Gibbins, R., & Walters, R. Three preliminary studies of a psychoanalytic theory of alcohol addiction. *Quarterly Journal of Studies on Alcohol*, 1960, *21*(4), 618-641.

Glass, S. J., Deuel, H. J., & Wright, C. A. Sex hormone studies in male homosexuality. *Endocrinology*, 1940, *26*(4), 590-594.

Goffman, E. *Stigma: Notes on the management of spoiled identity*. Englewood Cliffs, NJ: Prentice-Hall, 1963.

Goodwin, D. *Is alcoholism hereditary?* New York: Oxford University Press, 1976.

Goodwin, D. Alcoholism and heredity. *Archives of General Psychiatry*, 1979, *36*, 57-61.

Gusfield, J. *Symbolic crusade: Status politics and the American temperance movement*. Urbana: University of Illinois Press, 1963.

Hatterer, L. *Changing homosexuality in the male*. New York: McGraw-Hill, 1970.

Hawkins, J. Lesbianism and alcoholism. In M. Greenblatt & M. Schuckit (Eds.), *Alcoholism problems in women and children*. New York: Grune and Stratton, 1976.

Hills, S. *Demystifying social deviance*. New York: McGraw-Hill, 1980.

Hooker, E. Male homosexuals and their "worlds." In J. Marmor (Ed.), *Sexual inversion*. New York: Basic Books, 1965.

Judd, T. D. A survey of non-gay alcoholism treatment agencies and services offered for gay women and men. In D. Smith, S. Anderson, M. Buxton, N. Gottlieb, W. Harvey, & T. Chung (Eds.), *A multicultural view of drug abuse*. Cambridge, MA: G. K. Hall/Shenkman, 1978.

Kallmann, F. J. Comparative twin study of the genetic aspects of male homosexuality. *Journal of Nervous and Mental Disease*, 1952, *115*, 283-298.

Kessel, N., & Walton, H. *Alcoholism*. Baltimore: Penguin Books, 1965.

Lang, T. Studies in the genetic determination of homosexuality. *Journal of Nervous and Mental Disease*, 1940, *92*, 55-64.

Levy, R. The psychodynamic functions of alcohol. *Quarterly Journal of Studies on Alcohol*, 1958, *19*(4), 649-659.

Lohrenz, L., Connelly, J., Coyne, L., & Spare, K. Alcohol problems in several midwestern homosexual communities. *Journal of Studies on Alcohol*, 1978, *39*(11), 1959-1963.

Lolli, G. Alcoholism and homosexuality in Tennessee Williams' "Cat on a Hot Tin Roof." *Quarterly Journal of Studies on Alcohol*, 1956, *17*(3), 543-553.

MacAndrew, C., & Edgerton, R. *Drunken comportment*. Chicago: Aldine, 1969.

Machover, S., Puzzo, F., Machover, K., & Plumeau, F. Clinical and objective studies of personality variables in alcoholism: III. An objective study of homosexuality in alcoholism. *Quarterly Journal of Studies on Alcohol*, 1959, *20*(2), 528-542.

Maddox, G. Teenage drinking in the United States. In D. Pittman & C. Snyder (Eds.), *Society, culture, and drinking patterns.* New York: John Wiley, 1962.

Michael, J. *The gay drinking problem: There is a solution.* Minneapolis: CompCare Publications, 1976.

Michael, J. *Sober, clean and gay!* Minneapolis: CompCare Publications, 1977.

Nardi, P. M. Alcohol treatment and the non-traditional family structures of gays and lesbians. *Journal of Alcohol and Drug Education, 27*(2), in press.

Read, K. *Other voices: The style of a male homosexual tavern.* Novato, CA: Chandler and Sharp Publishers, 1980.

Robinson, D. *From drinking to alcoholism: A sociological commentary.* New York: John Wiley, 1976.

Roebuck, J., & Kessler, R. *The etiology of alcoholism.* Springfield, IL: Charles C. Thomas Publishers, 1972.

Room, R. Ambivalence as a sociological explanation: The case of cultural explanations of alcohol problems. *American Sociological Review,* 1976, *41*(6), 1047-1065.

Saghir, M., & Robins, E. *Male and female homosexuality.* Baltimore: Williams and Wilkins Co., 1973.

Sandmaier, M. *The invisible alcoholics: Women and alcohol abuse in America.* New York: McGraw-Hill, 1979.

Schuckit, M., & Haglund, R. An overview of the etiological theories on alcoholism. In N. Estes & E. Heinemann (Eds.), *Alcoholism: Development, consequences and interventions.* St. Louis: C. V. Mosby, 1977.

Schwartz, L. *Alcoholism among lesbians/gay men: A critical problem in critical proportions.* Phoenix: Do It Now Foundation, 1980.

Shilts, R. Alcoholism: A look in depth at how a national menace is affecting the gay community. *Advocate,* February 25, 1976, pp. 16-19; 22-25.

Small, E., & Leach, B. Counseling homosexual alcoholics. *Journal of Studies on Alcohol,* 1977, *38*(11), 2077-2086.

Snyder, C. Inebriety, alcoholism and anomie. In M. Clinard (Ed.), *Anomie and deviant behavior.* New York: Free Press, 1964.

Socarides, C. *The overt homosexual.* New York: Grune and Stratton, 1968.

Steffen, J., Steffen, V., & Nathan, P. Behavioral approaches to alcohol abuse. In N. Estes & E. Heinemann (Eds.), *Alcoholism: Development, consequences and interventions.* St. Louis: C. V. Mosby, 1977.

Szasz, T. *The manufacture of madness.* New York: Harper and Row, 1970.

Tahka, V. *The alcoholic personality: A clinical study.* Helsinki: Finnish Foundation for Alcohol Studies, 1966.

Trice, H. *Alcoholism in America.* New York: McGraw-Hill, 1966.

Ullman, A. Sociocultural backgrounds of alcoholism. *Annals of the American Academy of Political and Social Science,* 1958, *315,* 48-54.

Wallace, J. Alcoholism from the inside out: A phenomenological analysis. In N. Estes & E. Heinemann, (Eds.), *Alcoholism: Development, consequences, and interventions.* St. Louis: C. V. Mosby, 1977.

Warren C. *Identity and community in the gay world.* New York: John Wiley, 1974.

Weinberg, M., & Williams, C. *Male homosexuals.* New York: Oxford University Press, 1974.

West, D. J. *Homosexuality.* Chicago: Aldine, 1967.

Williams, T. *Cat on a hot tin roof.* New York: New Directions, 1955.

Wilson, E. *On human nature.* New York: Bantam Books, 1978.

Ziebold, T. *Alcoholism and the gay community.* Washington, D.C.: Whitman-Walker Clinic and Blade Communications, 1978.

Ziebold, T. Alcoholism and recovery: Gays helping gays. *Christopher Street,* January 1979, pp. 36-44.

WHO SHOULD BE DOING WHAT
ABOUT THE GAY ALCOHOLIC?

Tricia A. Zigrang, PhD

ABSTRACT. Treatment options for the homosexual alcoholic are examined with the conclusion that increased education for staff about the particular needs of homosexual alcoholics
and development of specialized services in existing treatment facilities are high priorities. A
description of the format of in-service training provided for one agency staff and the results
of the training are presented. Finally, directions for future research in the area of homosexual alcoholism are suggested.

The literature available on the prevalence of alcoholism among homosexual
men and women has been reviewed by Peter Nardi in the preceding article.
Directly applicable reports are summarized in Table 1. Others have arrived at
estimates of the prevalence of alcoholism in the gay community on the basis of
the utilization of services in gay community resource centers. Brenda Weathers,
after approximately three years of work at the Los Angeles Gay Community
Services Center, reports that an estimated 25 to 35% of the individuals who
came for services had a significant alcohol problem. (Shilts, 1976) Survey
interviews at gay counseling clinics in Pittsburgh and Philadelphia indicate that
33 to 50% of clients seeking help for other problems at these clinics are
actually suffering from alcoholism. (Ziebold, 1978)

Survey of Service Programs

With such documentation of the high rates of alcoholism, one becomes sur-
prised at the relative lack of response by both those in the area of alcoholism
treatment and those involved in gay counseling generally. There are very few
articles in the alcoholism literature on homosexual alcoholism. At a time when
alcohol services for special populations are being stressed (i.e., for youth,
women, the elderly, blacks, chicanos, and American Indians) there has been
almost no mention of specialized services for homosexual alcoholics.

Dr. Zigrang is currently in private practice in Portland, OR. Her present address is 11050 SW
16th Drive, Portland, OR 97219. This paper was presented at the National Council on Alcoholism
Annual Meeting in Seattle, Washington, May 1980.

Table 1. Studies of the Prevalence of
Alcoholism in Gay Populations

Year	Investigator	Number of Subjects	Alcohol Dependent
1970	Saghir et al	89 male	30%
1970	Saghir et al	57 female	35%
1974	Weinberg, Williams	2497 male	29%
1975	Fifield	--	31%
1978	Lohrenz et al	145 male	29%

Alcoholism appears to have been ignored by many of those working in the field of gay counseling and research as well. For example, at a National Symposium on Homosexuality (AASECT, Atlanta, GA, January 1980), alcoholism was not mentioned at all in a presentation titled "Homosexuality and Psychological Adjustment," and was mentioned only in passing, with no attempt to outline its significance to the gay community, in a presentation on "Gay Counseling: Its Present and Future Directions." Perhaps the most complete and extensive study of the psychological and social adaptation of homosexuals to date is that reported by Bell and Weinberg (1978) in their book *Homosexualities*. This book does not contain a single reference to alcoholism. It would seem that every important question pertaining to psychological and social adaptation was asked except "How much do you drink?"

As part of her investigation of alcoholism in the gay community in Los Angeles, Fifield (1975) surveyed personnel in 46 "nongay" agencies in Los Angeles County that provided services for alcoholics. She found that while 76% of the agencies acknowledge that "gay people have unique service needs," only two out of the 46 agencies reported having therapy groups specifically for gay clients, only 3 reported that they referred homosexuals to a gay agency, only 4 reported any effort to outreach to the homosexual alcoholic, and only 4 reported ever having conducted staff training to increase awareness of homosexual life-styles. The staff at these agencies estimated that only 1% of their alcoholic clientele is gay. This estimation becomes particularly significant when compared with a survey of participants in existing gay alcoholism programs in the area: 50% of these individuals stated that they had previously participated in nongay alcohol rehabilitation programs. It would seem that many gay alcoholics are not revealing their sexual orientation in the nongay treatment settings.

Because of our concern regarding the adequacy of treatment of the homosexual alcoholic by an inpatient unit in a Veterans Administration Medical Center (VAMC), an evaluation of that treatment was undertaken. In an inpatient program in which the primary therapeutic mode is group psychotherapy, the problem facing the homosexual alcoholic was thought to be the following:

> They are faced with the choice of whether or not to reveal their sexual orientation to fellow group members . . . nondisclosure results in the need to maintain considerable censorship and ultimately tends to result in radically decreased group participation; however, disclosure of their orientation is likely to result in considerable rejection and isolation from other group members.

This statement was included in a letter that detailed this dilemma and asked for information about handling of this particular problem and about different treatment approaches taken with the homosexual alcoholic; letters were sent in the summer of 1979 to 78 Alcohol Treatment Units located in VAMCs across the country. Replies were received from 32 VAMCs in 24 different states. A few of those responding said that they focused on drinking and saw little if any relevance of a patient's sexuality to drinking. Most said that they had no special programs, had only a few homosexual patients, and tended to address this issue in individual sessions if it was problematic for the patient. A few programs referred homosexual clients to gay community resources for treatment when these were available. Many programs reported that although disclosure of sexual orientation was infrequent, when individuals did make such a disclosure they were usually accepted by fellow patients. Several units reported that homosexuality and sexuality were areas with which they were uncomfortable and which they were not adequately addressing at present. A few had or were in the process of organizing in-service training in these areas.

One program's approach stood apart from all the others as exemplified by the following quotes from the respondent's description of the program:

> We have had many patients in our combined alcohol/drug 30-day inpatient unit reveal and discuss openly their homosexuality. They have not reported rejection and isolation from other group members, but have reported acceptance and involvement. . . . We have two sexuality lectures in our 20 lecture series and encourage all patients to discuss, examine, and develop their individual sexuality. If the individual is accepting of his homosexuality, we encourage participation in gay self-help groups while still in treatment and openness in group about his sexuality and its impact on daily living. If the individual is uncertain or anxious about his sexual orientation, we discuss it individually and neither encourage nor discourage discussion in group.

To generalize from the responses of the facilities in these two separate surveys, one might conclude that either relatively few homosexual alcoholics are seeking treatment or that many are not disclosing their sexual orientation when in treatment. One might also conclude that there appears to be little awareness on the part of most treatment facilities of the special needs of the homosexual alcoholic and little attempt to familiarize staff of these treatment facilities with the gay life-style and those aspects of it which are particularly important in treatment efforts.

In light of the above, it is easy to understand why some individuals question the ability of most agencies to reach and treat their gay clients and suggest that the gay community must accept responsibility for helping gay alcoholics. Ziebold (1978) one of the leading proponents of increased involvement on the part of the gay community in combatting homosexual alcoholism, gives the following reasons for his stance: (1) The gay alcoholic is less likely to have a supportive family structure (spouse, children, parents and other relatives) to help her/him in efforts to stop drinking and thus desperately needs a sense of a caring community or surrogate "family." The gay community could provide such support. (2) Intervention to halt the active drinking stage has to be brought into the gay community to increase the chance of reaching the socially isolated homosexual and to remove the threat of exposing one's orientation. (3) Effective treatment for the gay alcoholic requires a setting that provides a drug-free re-entry into social relationships within the gay community when that is the individual's preferred life-style. Such a re-entry would be maximized by treatment in a gay-oriented setting. (4) Recovery of the gay alcoholic needs to emphasize self-acceptance as a homosexual and as a member of the homosexual subculture. A gay community treatment center would provide the essential role models for a mature homosexual life-style. Ziebold concludes, "If the gay community doesn't provide help for gay alcoholics, no one else is going to do it" (p. 6).

While Ziebold's arguments for gay community involvement in combatting gay alcoholism and ultimately for gay community operated treatment facilities are both compelling and valid, there are inherent difficulties in this approach. First, only a few of the largest cities have gay communities sufficiently organized to launch and support such intervention efforts. Second, chronic alcoholism contributes to severe physical deterioration and is often accompanied by various medical disabilities. As a result, many chronic alcohol abusers are best treated in a medical setting where they can receive treatment for their physical as well as psychological and social problems. The cost of establishing new medical facilities to serve only gay clients would be high and only in larger cities is there likely to be a large enough gay population to justify separate facilities. Thus homosexuals in smaller and midsize communities would still be required to seek treatment from available "nongay" treatment facilities. Third, such an approach continues to separate and isolate the homosexual from the larger, predominantly heterosexual environment. Such separation may be beneficial initially, but ultimately will continue to reinforce the homosexual's feelings of alienation from the majority and will also allow heterosexual staff and patients to continue to avoid an examination of their own feelings and attitudes toward homosexuals. If gay alcoholic treatment facilities are available, it may be easier to refer homosexual clients than to make such introspection. Increased understanding of homosexuals by heterosexuals is needed in order to combat the homophobic attitudes that have likely contributed to homosexual alcoholism. Such understanding can only be gained through increased communication and contact between the two groups. Thus, while gay community operated treatment facilities for alcoholism have many advantages in the treatment of homosexual alcoholism, their primary disadvantage may be that through their separation from the heterosexual majority they may ultimately contribute to the perpetuation of homophobic attitudes that appear to have significantly contributed to gay alcoholism in the first place.

Development of Specific Program

In view of the limitations the gay community is likely to face in setting up alcoholism treatment facilities for gay clients, providing further education for staff members in existing alcohol treatment facilities regarding homosexual alcoholism, the gay life-style, and the development of specialized services for gay clients should be a high priority. Such an attempt at further education was made on a VAMC Alcohol Treatment Unit. The following is a description of the in-service training format utilized and the results of these sessions. The first sessions opened with the showing of the film *Gay, Proud and Sober* which is a sensitive documentary that examines the needs of the alcoholic in the gay community.[1] The film proceeds from the premise that a homosexual's affirmation of his sexuality can be used as a valuable tool to help him develop self-respect and make the critical personal decisions required in the process of rejecting dependence on alcohol. In addition, the session leaders summarized the major points about alcoholism and homosexuality in the recent literature and reported responses from other VAMCs regarding their treatment of the gay alcoholic. For the second session, several members of the local gay AA group were invited to speak to the staff about their own experiences and in particular were asked to discuss their own views of the relationship between homosexuality and alcoholism and of treatment approaches to the homosexual alcoholic. For the third session, an interested member of the gay community spoke to the staff about the psychological aspects of the gay life-style and about the difficulties he had encountered in his previous attempts to work with

---

[1]The film "Gay, Proud, and Sober" is available through Southerby Productions, 1709 E. 28th Street, Long Beach, CA 90806, Code 4109.

mental health professionals. These in-service training sessions were accompanied by many informal talks among staff members about homosexual alcoholism and by circulation of relevant literature.

Upon conclusion of these training sessions a re-examination of the unit's treatment approach to the homosexual alcoholic was undertaken. It was felt that the homosexual alcoholic applying for treatment on a VAMC alcohol unit faced problems different from any other minority group. Perhaps one of the most significant problems stems from the mental health professional's past labeling of homosexuality as a disorder. While this stance has recently been changed, many homosexuals are unaware of this change and others have already had negative experiences with therapists who have seen homosexuality as pathological or who have tried to change the client's sexual orientation. Thus, homosexual patients may have certain expectations of the type of treatment they will receive should they reveal their homosexuality. These expectations lead to decreased disclosure of sexual orientation to therapists and severely impair the establishment of a therapeutic alliance, inhibiting the therapist's understanding of the individual and of the particular factors that contribute to his drinking problem. Those applying for treatment in a government facility may have even more reason to be wary about disclosure of their sexuality, as they are well aware of the military's attitude toward homosexuals exemplified by the policy statement of the United States Senate, Article 921, 1966:

> It is the policy of the Department of the Army that homosexual personnel will not be permitted to serve in the Army in any capacity; prompt separation of homosexuals is mandatory. The Army considers homosexuals to be unfit for military service because their presence impairs the morale and discipline of the Army, and that homosexuality is a manifestation of a severe personality defect which appreciably limits the ability of such individuals to function in society.

Homosexuals seeking treatment at government sponsored facilities such as VAMCs may fear that disclosure of their sexuality will somehow result in termination of their present military benefits and make them ineligible for any further treatment at such a facility.

Even if a homosexual alcoholic should choose to share his orientation with a therapist on a typical VAMC unit, he is still faced with the choice of whether or not to reveal his sexuality to fellow patients. Most alcoholics have greatly lowered self-esteem as a result of their drinking behavior. It can be hypothesized that as a result of the antihomosexual attitude prevalent in society, the self-esteem of homosexual alcoholics is even further impaired. They may feel so badly about themselves that they would be reluctant to be open about their sexual orientation in a predominantly heterosexual group, fearing rejection and isolation. Attempting to hide or disguise their orientation leads to decreased group participation, decreased openness and ultimately prevents them from receiving the help they need in order to increase self-esteem and maintain sobriety.

In view of the problems described above, it was determined by a majority of the staff on the VAMC Alcohol treatment unit that the addition of an outpatient group limited to homosexual alcoholics only would improve the treatment with this particular segment of the alcoholic population. It was felt that such a group would help alleviate some of the aforementioned difficulties by providing a less threatening atmosphere where the homosexual alcoholic would be more comfortable both in discussing daily problems and in coming to terms with any negative feelings about his homosexuality. It was also hoped that publicly addressing this issue would dispel the homosexual alcoholic's possible perceptions that mental health personnel are unwilling or unable to treat alcoholics with this sexual orientation. Homosexuals utilizing the in-patient program were to be placed in mixed heterosexual/homosexual groups since one of the ultimate goals was for homosexuals to relate comfortably with heterosexuals.

For those in the inpatient groups, the outpatient group could serve as a place to sort out the advantages and disadvantages of being open about their sexuality with fellow patients. Permission to hold such a group was granted in December 1979.

Another result of these sessions was that a female staff member who had been working on the unit since October 1972 for the first time publicly revealed her homosexual orientation to the rest of the staff.[2] She had previously been reluctant to do so, fearing both a termination of her employment and possible rejection by some staff members. Many staff members had previously suspected her orientation, but most had not spoken directly to her about this. Her self-disclosure was thought to be an important step in improving treatment for gay alcoholics on the unit. Patients tend to model staff behavior, and if the staff cannot deal openly with and accept a fellow staff member's homosexuality, patients can hardly be expected to do so.

The above staff member became co-leader of the homosexual outpatient group as it was felt important to have a gay non-alcoholic role model. The group has been functioning for several months with mixed success. The most pervasive problem at present is in getting those people who are eligible for the group to attend an initial session. Several of the individuals who were appropriate candidates for the group were so conflicted about their sexuality that participation in such a group was too threatening. Several have expressed concern about others finding out about their participation in such a group. Another inhibiting factor to the so far exclusively male homosexual population

---

[2]In our experience this is not uncommon. One of the first tangible results of an agency's publicizing its concern about and receptiveness to the needs of homosexual clients is often self-disclosure of homosexuality by some members of the staff to other staff members (Editors' note).

could be the presence of two female co-therapists. While the importance of a male therapist was recognized, two females were chosen since the staff member who initiated training and changes in this area and who is the most familiar with problems facing the gay alcoholic is female and the only homosexual staff member is also female.

While the group has been limited in attendance, several individuals who have participated reported finding the group beneficial. They expressed initial concerns about the purpose of the group, citing the military's well-known stance on homosexuality. One member shared his military experiences regarding his homosexuality, recounting that when it was discovered he was gay he was given the choice of a discharge or going to front line combat. One of the most common themes of the group to date has been difficulties in reconciling their homosexuality with various religious doctrines. Many of the individuals in the group came from highly religious backgrounds that emphasized homosexual immorality and unnaturalness. Such proclamations appear to have created more uncertainty and difficulties for these individuals than any other form of anti-homosexual statements. Other topics included finding alternative support systems when individuals are rejected by their family or friends because of their sexuality, finding alternatives to the gay bar for socializing, and sorting out the advantages and disadvantages of "coming out" to friends, family, employers, and others.

Conclusions

These descriptions of one staff member's efforts to provide in-service training on gay alcoholism and the results of these efforts support the contention that training and education can alter the treatment that gay alcoholics presently receive in predominantly heterosexual treatment facilities. These treatment efforts need to be continually evaluated and revised to provide the most effective treatment for this population.

Equally necessary for improved treatment of the gay alcoholic is further research regarding those factors contributing to the high prevalence of alcoholism among homosexuals, a prevalence rate more than adequately documented by a series of studies. Nevertheless, explanations for the high rate represent conjecture only. One way in which possible contributing factors to gay alcoholism could be identified would be to compare gay alcoholics with gay non-alcoholics on a number of important dimensions. Examination of the differences between these two groups may be helpful in indicating causal factors in gay alcoholism.

A look at Bell and Weinberg's (1978) investigations suggests other important areas to be examined. As previously mentioned, one dimension which Bell and Weinberg *failed* to investigate in their comprehensive study was drinking behavior.[3] It would be interesting and informative to know if there are different levels of alcohol usage in the different typologies identified by these authors. For example, is the well adjusted "Functional" who spends considerable time in gay bars more likely to develop a drinking problem than the lonely, uninvolved "Asexual" who seldom goes to gay bars or *vice versa*? Studies which compare gay alcoholics with gay nonalcoholics on these different dimensions are needed to answer these questions. Such answers may have important implications for treatment of this population.

In summary, the documentation of extensive alcoholism in the gay community calls for action on the part of alcoholism treatment professionals and of researchers and gay counselors. Increased awareness of this problem is necessary, along with attempts to improve services to gay alcoholic clients and to isolate and curb those factors contributing to the high prevalence of alcoholism in the gay community.

REFERENCES

Bell, A., & Weinberg, M. *Homosexualities: A study of diversity among men and women*. New York: Simon and Schuster, 1978.

Fifield, L. *On my way to nowhere*. Los Angeles: Gay Community Services Center, 1975.

Shilts, R. Alcoholism: A Look in depth at how a national menace is affecting the gay community. *Advocate*, Feb 25, 1976, 16-19, 22-25.

Ziebold, T. O. *Alcoholism and the gay community*. Washington, DC: Blade Communications, Inc., 1978.

---

[3]Bell and Weinberg also did not investigate other drug use, in spite of being concerned with social behavior of an urban population. (Editors' note).

THE TIES THAT BIND:
STRATEGIES FOR COUNSELING
THE GAY MALE CO-ALCOHOLIC

Scott Whitney

ABSTRACT. Within the gay male subculture, strong pressures strengthen the ties between the gay male alcoholic and emotionally significant other persons in his life. This article is an attempt to describe a theoretical model for viewing co-addiction with a more specific discussion of how this model applies to gay male relationships. The brief theoretical discussion is followed by a discussion of common presenting complaints of gay co-alcoholics and a more detailed treatment of counseling strategies, from initial contact to participation in support programs, that have proven effective in an outpatient setting.

Little enough specialized clinical work is being done with gay male alcoholics and still less is known about working with their alcoholic lovers. The field of alcoholism treatment has seen an assimilation in the last 10 years of the ideas developed by family therapy practitioners and the folk wisdom of Alcoholics Anonymous which, through its support of Al-Anon family groups, has emphasized the needs of those in relationships with the alcoholic. But what, precisely, constitutes the "family group" for the gay male alcoholic, and what unique aspects of gay relationships should treatment personnel be aware of when attempting to facilitate recovery from alcoholism?

Defining Co-Alcoholism

Basically, the co-alcoholic is a person in the alcoholic's life who intervenes in such a way as to prevent the alcoholic from facing the consequences of his actions. This rescuing behavior involves the gradual assumption, sometimes over the course of years, of responsibility for finances, social life, and vocational matters. The co-alcoholic is always the person at the front door negotiating with reality while the alcoholic is allowed to continue his toxic abdication of responsibility. Once this pattern is in place, of course, it creates a deeply ingrained *folie à deux* in which the co-alcoholic begins to share such

Scott Whitney was Coordinator of Men's Services with the Whitman-Radclyffe Foundation in San Francisco. His current address is P.O. Box 584, Eastsound, WA 98245.

alcoholic symptoms as denial, low self-esteem, depression, social isolation, and high anxiety states.

If treatment personnel are to adopt a whole-system intervention when working with the gay male alcoholic, they must begin to look very closely at the social support system that has maintained the addiction. Implicit in the alcoholic's recovery is the fact that his social support system will be disrupted and that systems of this sort have a way of trying to restore their own equilibrium, sometimes at the expense of the alcoholic's sobriety.

In mainstream culture, the co-alcoholic role is usually maintained by a husband or wife. With gay male alcoholics, a wider range of social roles is involved which requires close scrutiny before attempting intervention. If the alcoholic is in a coupled relationship, the lover is the most likely candidate for the co-alcoholic role. When the client is single, however, any number of people in his life might be serving this function. Since adopting a whole-system approach, our agency has discovered that the co-alcoholic role can be filled by an ex-wife, clergyman, employer, roommate, sibling, mother, father, co-worker, or (not at all uncommon) a therapist. The following is a short example of a non-lover co-alcoholic relationship:

> A 37-year-old gay male alcoholic presented himself for treatment. After some discussion, it was unclear to the counselor why the man had not been fired from his job because of his numerous binges and institutional detoxifications that had involved much time away from work. Further exploration revealed that the man's employer was a closeted homosexual who maintained a wife, family, and a straight social identity. Our client was important to this man as both a drinking buddy and as a contact in the gay subculture. The employer was thus willing to make any allowances needed, including monetary, to keep our client close to him. It became obvious that intervention in this self-regulating system would be necessary to facilitate our client's progress in recovery.

Common Co-Alcoholic Issues

From a longitudinal point of view, we have discovered that many gay male co-alcoholics have an alcoholic parent. This means that they have learned early in life the intricacies of rescuing, denial, and guilt. For some, it seems to be necessary for their own self-esteem to have an alcoholic in their lives. Even those co-alcoholics who have not experienced alcoholism in their family backgrounds admit, after some time in treatment, that they became involved with the alcoholic at a time in their lives when they were at some transition point and felt depressed, helpless, or disoriented. In some cases a kind of bipolar oscillation has occurred in which the alcoholic, at an earlier stage of addiction, played parent to the co-alcoholic as child.

If the co-alcoholic re-establishes himself as autonomous, then the alcoholism of the other partner begins to worsen. Conversely, this pattern accounts for the frequently noted phenomenon of the alcoholic's lover exhibiting symptoms when the alcoholic begins the recovery process. This makes "family" intervention imperative if the relationship is to stabilize during recovery.

Sometimes there are hidden sexual agendas in these relationships. The co-alcoholic partner may be older or overweight or may in some way feel less attractive than the alcoholic. When this is the case, there is a great fear on the part of the co-alcoholic that if the alcoholic sobers up, he will see his partner in a new light and seek someone else. In other cases, the two partners disagree on preferred sexual activity, and it is only when the alcoholic is drunk that he permits, for instance, anal intercourse. Alcoholics in the initial stages of recovery many times experience impotence, and this can also be a source of strain on the relationship. When any of the above dynamics is present, there is a vested interest on the part of the co-alcoholic in the continuation of the alcoholics drinking behavior. Dealing with these issues requires that the counselor be comfortable with discussing homosexuality and have the skills necessary to create a safe environment for the disclosure of crucial issues.

In our experience, the majority of gay male co-alcoholic tends to be high-achieving, workaholic, Type-A personalities who have few sources of support and who lead highly compartmentalized lives. They manifest many symptoms including insomnia, anxiety attacks, overeating, ulcers, headaches, depression, and sexual dysfunction. In terms of interpersonal relations, they tend toward a generalized shell-shock syndrome which seems to be the result of long exposure to the unpredictable and arbitrary reactions of the alcoholic partner. They have learned to adapt to an ever-changing interpersonal environment which requires them constantly to change both the process and the content of communication depending on the shifting state of mind of the alcoholic. Co-alcoholics learn to communicate in one way when the alcoholic is sober, in another when he is drunk, and in still another when he is hung-over. Some have described this as a feeling of "walking on eggs" around the alcoholic. This shell shock continues even after the alcoholic has achieved abstinence. A primary goal in treating the co-alcoholic is retraining him to give direct, consistent messages regardless of the changing moods of the alcoholic.

Strategies for Treatment

The counselor must first be aware that co-alcoholics are very difficult to bring into treatment and that progress is slow and difficult to evaluate. The co-alcoholic fears three things most of all about entering treatment. The first is that he will be blamed for the alcoholic's condition. Indeed, most co-alcoholics have already blamed themselves and fear further accusations of failure. The second fear is that the goal of treatment will be to disengage them from their relationship. Many recognize that there are few logical reasons for them to have remained with the alcoholic and have even received feedback from friends regarding the futility of maintaining the relationship. The question "Why do you stay with him?" is fraught with implications of personal inadequacy on the part of the co-alcoholic. If the co-alcoholic is also a drinker or uses other drugs, he will additionally fear a third possibility: that he will be confronted with his own addictive patterns. Even if the counselor suspects addiction in the co-alcoholic, the usual guidelines of confrontation and breaking down of denial must be set aside, at least temporarily, in order to get him into treatment. When more rapport has been established, this issue can be approached in a non-threatening manner, and (as is many times the case) the co-alcoholic can be guided into treatment for his own addictions.

Sometimes the initial contact with the treatment agency is made by the co-alcoholic. When this is the case, the counselor should use the opportunity to provide as much information as possible concerning treatment for the alcoholic as well as information on co-alcoholism and Al-Anon. One phone call may be the only opportunity for intervention.

When the alcoholic is the first to be seen by the agency, we have been successful in getting the lover to attend an initial interview by telling the alcoholic that the agency requires his partner to come in for at least one appointment to share information on the disease of alcoholism and to see how he can help in the recovery process. Suggesting that there are things to learn about helping the alcoholic hooks into the co-alcoholic's ever-present need to be of assistance to his partner and facilitates the likelihood of his making an appointment. Confidentiality is a major issue, and it must be emphasized to both parties that their disclosures will be protected from outside sources and from each other.

Gay Co-Alcoholics in Therapy Groups

Ideally, the initial contact is followed by several individual sessions which serve to prepare the client for entrance into a co-alcoholic group. While recovery from co-addiction is usually considered a two- to four-year process, talking in terms of such a prolonged time-frame can be discouraging. We usually approach this issue by requesting that the client try coming to a meeting (not a therapy group) once a week for a month. A commitment can usually be negotiated on this basis with the hope that, once involved, the newcomer will form ties with other group members and remain in the group much longer.

Groups should be kept small (no more than six participants), and an atmosphere that is informational, open, and nonconfrontive must be maintained. For many clients, this is their first chance to socialize with other gay men, and in this way the group becomes a first step out of the social isolation so common among gay co-alcoholics. A natural tendency, at least initially, is for members of such groups to spend a great deal of time blaming their partners. This tendency can be gently extinguished by the facilitator's focusing on the issues group members must face for themselves. Clients should be encouraged to exchange phone numbers and to socialize outside the group. This gives them the chance to develop social skills that will enhance self-esteem and facilitate the likelihood of their developing support for themselves outside of their toxic relationships.

Because of the kinds of symptoms manifested by co-alcoholics, we have found that educating them on concepts of stress and stress management seems to be very beneficial for symptom amelioration. Additionally, doing relaxation, meditation, and fantasy exercises with the group creates an atmosphere in which they can relax enough to begin to play. For most of them, the element of play has been absent from their lives for years.

At the beginning of treatment, many co-alcoholic clients are pessimistic about relationships in general and about gay life in particular. As involvement in the group continues, many find themselves achieving a positive gay identity, perhaps for the first time.

Because they live in what is still considered by society a deviant subculture, it has become easy for co-alcoholics to adopt the role of victim. Their involvement with a practicing alcoholic has reinforced this role and encouraged the idea that they must protect their weaker partner. Before entering treatment, they feel themselves not only separated from mainstream society but also cut off from the potential support of their subculture. Gay friends outside the relationship have been discarded because of embarrassment and shame over the alcoholic's behavior. Working in a small group format is a powerful means of overcoming the victim identity and reconnecting clients to the genuine potential for support which exists within the gay community.

Conclusion

Treatment personnel must look closely at the social system supporting the addictions of their gay male clients. It is important that those who serve in a co-alcoholic role within that system be contacted and, if possible, brought into treatment.

Working in small group formats that emphasize alcohol education, stress management, communication skills, and increased socialization within the gay community has proved effective in an outpatient setting. Clients should be encouraged to involve themselves in Al-Anon both as a means of deepening their knowledge of co-addiction and as a means of strengthening their own support system.

COUNSELING THE HOMOSEXUAL ALCOHOLIC

Ronnie W. Colcher, MSW

ABSTRACT. The author summarizes her clinical experience with 75 homosexual alcoholics, 47 male and 28 female, of diverse backgrounds. Similarities and differences in treating homosexual and heterosexual alcoholics are presented. A summary of recommendations for the counselor working with homosexual alcoholics is included.

Significant numbers of homosexual alcoholics should be offered services in social agencies and private practice. For many reasons, overt and covert, they are falling into the cracks of the service delivery system. Two reasons for this may be that social service providers are reluctant around alcoholism and are fearful about homosexuality. Counseling people who are "different" is only difficult when one does not have knowledge of and is not sensitive to their uniqueness as well as their similarities.

This paper begins with the gay[1] alcoholic coming for treatment. Though the different theories of causality of either homosexuality or alcoholism will not be discussed, they have been recognized in the preparation of this article. For purposes of this paper, alcoholism is defined as an illness characterized by significant impairment that is directly associated with persistent and excessive use of alcohol. In addition, impairment may involve psychological, physiological, or social dysfunction (American Medical Association, 1977, p. 4). Homosexuality is defined here as "simply the nature of a person's sexual object choice for another person of the same sex" (Bell, 1976, p. 202). Bell says that homosexuality is so diverse, the variety of its psychological, social, and sexual correlates so enormous, its originating factors so numerous, that to use the term to mean anything more than that is misleading.

Although Mary Richmond recognized the need for special services and treatment for alcoholics as far back as 1917, the field is relatively new. There are nevertheless a few areas of agreement. Most psychodynamically oriented therapists as well as those in the field of alcoholism agree that focusing on under-

Mrs. Colcher is Director of the Alcoholism Program at the Valley Forge Medical Center and Hospital, Norristown, Pennsylvania.

[1]In this paper the word "gay" will be used interchangeably with the word "homosexual." The term is preferred in popular use.

lying causes does not work. There is general agreement that the role of the therapist must be more active and directive than analytical while still being nonjudgmental. In the beginning, because the patient may be so overwhelmed by reality and its demands, treatment is usually limited to sustainment, ventilation, and alleviation of concrete environmental needs; short periods of silence frequently employed to increase anxiety should be monitored carefully so that the level of tension does not become so high that the patient discontinues treatment. This does not mean that the alcoholic patient should be overprotected. The rationalizations and denial must be confronted initially or there is little chance the patient will take responsibility for his behavior and see how dysfunctional it is. This requires a delicate balance of facing the drinking problem and communicating faith that it can be overcome (Snyder, 1975). To do this, a relationship of trust must be established.

Until very recently, homosexuality was considered a pathological state, and it is still not really accepted by the larger society. Even more than the alcoholic, the homosexual tends to be viewed with disdain, fear, mistrust, and ignorance by western society. In response to this social negativism, there is a tendency for a homosexual to be a self-oppressor.

With the change in the concept of homosexuality from a disease to one of sexual preference, homosexuals with increasing frequency began to seek treatment for problems other than their homosexuality. Many therapists, covertly if not overtly, still see homosexuality as the major problem. There is some controversy among therapists as to what to do when a patient's sexual orientation differs from their own. The basic questions are whether to attempt to treat, to refer, or not even to refer.

A homosexual coming for treatment should be treated as anyone else with his particular problem. Many forms of therapy may be used depending on the needs and desires of that unique individual. In no way should even a subtle push to change someone's sexual orientation be condoned. One should be sensitive to the needs of the client, whether he is gay or not. Some clinicians enumerate sensitive areas for gays, among which are feeling "different" and "alone." The gay person is often tempted to dull this pain by the misuse of drugs or alcohol. Because of society's view of homosexuality and the gay persons's view of self, initially he or she may not be very trusting. When trust develops, the client can become extremely vulnerable. Sensitivity to gays in existing facilities for alcoholics is necessary so that patients can open up about conflicts related to or concealed by alcoholism. It is also important to incorporate personnel who specialize in alcoholism into gay health agencies. Alcoholics Anonymous has included the gay and lesbian alcoholic in its literature along with other minority groups (Alcoholics Anonymous, 1976). One medical company has published two pamphlets which are very much like the traditional AA literature but which use gay histories for their basis (Michael, 1976; 1977). Although there has been a modest increase in articles in the professional literature, there has been little to help the counselor who is working with gay alcoholics. Because of this, I turned to my own clinical experience, to individuals in gay social service organizations, and to gay AA to formulate a recommended treatment approach.

Clinical Experience

During the last 7 years, I have worked with 75 homosexual alcoholics; 62 were initially seen as inpatients in an alcohol detoxification unit in a general hospital, the Valley Forge Medical Center and Hospital, Norristown, Pennsylvania. Some returned for additional counseling after initial treatment was completed and more sobriety attained. The distribution of clients by gender and race is given in Table 1.

The hospital detoxification unit usually has about 1500 admissions per year; each of the 62 known gay inpatients was admitted an average of twice during the 7-year period. The patients ranged broadly in age and socioeconomic background. Formal education ranged from the fourth grade to the doctorate level. Their homosexual activities varied as did their drinking patterns, although two major groupings appeared in initial interviews.

(1) The homosexual alcoholics who are comfortable with their homosexuality. At first most patients fell into this category. The reasons for this are based on what they believed the counselor wanted to hear; what they wanted to tell the counselor; and, because of heavy drinking, what they really didn't know. This group, as time passed in treatment, talked about problems related to their homosexuality. Some individuals take a long time of testing the counseling relationship before they will talk openly about their feelings.

One patient, a 33-year-old white male, stated that he had no problems regarding his homosexuality. He was well educated and had a good job and a stable relationship with his lover. After being sober almost a year,

Table 1. Known Homosexual Alcoholics
Treated in Six Years 1974 Through 1980

	Male	Female	Total
White	30	18	48
Black	4	3	7
Hispanic	3	2	5
Total	37	23	60

he began to talk about his feelings of being alone. When asked when these had started, he said at the age of 6. This was when he had his first homosexual experience. He continued his homosexual relationships, and by the time he was 12 the feeling of loneliness was overwhelming.

As he began to recognize the historic relationship between his loneliness and his homosexuality as an appropriate area for exploration, the client began to see it as a problem and to discuss it with his counselor. A good basic rule is that if in the initial interview no problem is verbalized in this area, don't push. When rapport has been established and the patient is ready, he will tell you. Sobriety must be stressed first.

(2) The homosexual alcoholics who feel that their homosexuality is as much a problem as their alcoholism. This group usually has many other problems as well, which form a web so tight that the person is almost immobilized. When they find someone to whom they can finally talk, they want to tell everything at once.

A 38-year-old black lesbian stated that her homosexuality had always been a problem; growing up she was different. She married, thinking that it would change her. Her husband left her when he found out she was lesbian, and now she felt that her homosexuality was destroying her relationship with her son. She had never talked to anyone about this situation before.

It was important in this case to recognize the problem but not to let too much be said until there was time for trust to build. The interview focused on her alcoholism and how that was affecting her relationship with her son.

In both these groups, sobriety comes first. Sexuality is only disturbing if the counselor or client makes it so. The gay alcoholic, like any other alcoholic, is concerned with what he did and with what will happen. Until a person has achieved sobriety, it is difficult for the worker to discuss deeper issues and impossible for the patient to handle them. This does not mean that the counselor should not be aware of and sensitive to the client's homosexuality, simply that he or she should not treat homosexuality any differently than such factors as age, sex, race, religion, and national origin.

Treatment Similarities

Counseling the homosexual alcoholic is similar in many ways to counseling the heterosexual alcoholic. Sobriety is the primary goal. Taking Disulfiram (Antabuse, TM) is required by me for all outpatients unless medically contraindicated. The counselor is active and directive in the beginning. "Bread and butter" problems, such as medical attention, housing, unemployment, and welfare benefits, are priorities. Related to sobriety are problems around loneliness and structuring leisure time activities. These are major difficulties for most recovering alcoholics. They have isolated themselves by drinking, and the void must be filled. Alcoholics Anonymous can fill a part of that void. Many gay alcoholics are comfortable in these groups, although others feel the need for meetings where they can be more open about their homosexuality. Gay AA fills that need and also functions as a social activity for many.

Because of the importance of the gay bars for some members of the gay community as a primary place for dancing, cruising, and conversation, it is not unusual for a group of nondrinking alcoholics to go to a gay bar after an AA meeting. Coming from a background where a conservative treatment approach supported the philosophy that a recovering alcoholic should not go to bars, I was alarmed by this practice when I first began to work with gay alcoholics. When a patient goes to a bar with a nondrinking group to provide support, bar-going is not necessarily an obstacle to recovery. It is wise for the counselor to monitor the impact of this in each case, however.

Cruising for sexual pickups is also an area of concern for the recovering gay alcoholic. It does not appear to be where or when a person cruises, but the impact it has. If the person is constantly getting into situations that are degrading, tension-producing, or in conflict with the law, this may become a roadblock to recovery. It may also be indicative of a deeper problem, such as the compulsive need for a risk-laden experience. Sobriety may also bring sexual problems to many gay individuals. These problems usually clear up on their own except when alcohol has been used to reduce sexual inhibitions. The problem is not any different from the excessive use of alcohol for similar purposes by heterosexual clients.

The gay alcoholic has other social resources that are not alcohol oriented. The baths are frequently used as a sexual resource by gay men, but many times the additional pressure of competition is keen. There are many gay organizations: political (National Gay Task Force, Gay Rights National Lobby); religious (Dignity, for Catholics; and Beth'Achava, a Jewish group); professional (gay Social Workers, Nurses, etc.); and social (gay community centers). There are also a gay Mensa and many male and female discussion groups for those who want these activities. Around metropolitan areas there are numerous resources for gay alcoholics who want part or all of their lives involved with homosexual activities. Gay alcoholics living in rural areas have additional unique problems to which the counselor must be sensitive. If there are limited activities available, the patient may need more support. This may be achieved by contacting urban gay AA groups who will keep in touch by telephone.

In counseling the recovering gay alcoholic, one may become involved in couples counseling. This is not very different from counseling the heterosexual couple. When one member has come out and openly acknowledged his or her homosexuality and the other has not, there are problems similar to those seen in family services in mixed-religion or mixed-race marriages. If the roles are satisfactory to both parties, there are no problems. If not, then the expectations of each must be explored in therapy. For example, a problem for one lesbian couple was that one partner wanted a monogamous relationship and the other did not. Time had to be spent exploring their roles in that relationship.

Treatment Differences

As a rule, homosexuals fear coming into alcoholism treatment more than heterosexuals. This appears to be because of a fear of rejection by the facility, by the staff, and by other patients. Rather than view the counselor as someone who can help, the gay patient assumes that the counselor will not understand. If the counselor presents himself or herself in a warm, nonjudgmental way regarding homosexuality, the situation can be turned around. Sometimes, however, the patient will reveal too much:

> One 54-year-old white Catholic male was admitted for alcoholism. He was so relieved to have someone to talk to that he began to tell about his present life as a male prostitute as well as about having been raped throughout his childhood by his uncle. His parents knew nothing of the situation. After the father's death when the patient was 20, the uncle took over financial responsibility for the patient's mother. She lives in the uncle's house. The patient hates his uncle for what he did, yet he cannot support his mother on his own.

In this case, the counselor made the mistake of allowing the patient to say too much. The patient then felt guilty about how much of his background he had revealed, and the next sessions had to be spent working through the guilt. Had this been an outpatient setting, the mistake could have been disastrous, and he probably would never have returned to treatment.

The gay alcoholic has the additional social pressure of belonging to two groups not generally accepted by society. He/she must relate to four groups: nonalcoholic heterosexuals, alcoholic heterosexuals, nonalcoholic homosexuals, and alcoholic homosexuals.

> One gay alcoholic male seen in therapy experienced a great deal of difficulty on the job because of his co-workers' feelings about homosexuals. The conditions became so intolerable to him that he began to develop symptoms of acute anxiety. After many discussions he decided it was best to seek employment elsewhere. He has successfully been working in his new job for nine months. This man was neither militant nor active in any gay political groups which influenced his choice. Had he been, the purpose of counseling might have been very different, i.e., staying on the job and fighting it out.

Some gay alcoholics have difficulty relating to nongay AA meetings because of the pressure they feel to watch what they say. Indeed, some members of AA have been intolerant of the gay alcoholic. Other gay alcoholics have difficulty relating to nonalcoholic homosexual friends, since the stigma of alcoholism is as great in the gay community as elsewhere. This was explored in a discussion with a director of a gay switchboard, who said that the switchboard received few calls for problems about alcohol. Calls came in concerning problems with the law, finances, and social situations. The denial system of all alcoholics is so great that they really believe they would stop drinking so much if their other problems were solved. Their tendency, therefore, is to present their other problems and to ignore their drinking. When I first went to a gay bookstore and asked for popular literature that included alcoholism, very little was to be found. After several hours of searching, a very helpful woman began to talk about the avoidance of any mention of alcoholism. She told me that alcoholism is denied in the gay community as elsewhere (Olshan, Note 1).

Self-oppression, both in terms of alcoholism and homosexuality, frequently inhibits recovery. Having a patient read in either or both areas and discuss the material during interviews is helpful. It can also be important to have him list how he feels about alcoholism and homosexuality and how he thinks the rest of the world feels. Humor about oneself is a good indication of how far a patient has come in treatment. The humor can represent a healthy self-concept in perspective with the rest of the world.

Two areas where the counselor should take time and remain extremely passive in helping with decision-making are (1) "coming out"[2] and (2) questions around what to put on job applications or to say at job interviews about either homosexuality or alcoholism. Some people in AA feel one must be totally honest. Some feel it is not necessary to discuss these issues with prospective employers. The counselor can raise issues or act as a sounding board, but the implications are too great to try to influence the patient. Employers may consider alcoholism and homosexuality negatively in their hiring practices, and the individual must make the decision himself after weighing the alternatives. If one thinks of the alcoholic as having the same problems as other people only more so, then the problems of the gay alcoholic increase geometrically. Gay people also face special conflicts when they feel they can't come out fully and are guilty because they haven't.

This does not make sobriety and comfort in life an impossible goal, however, and counseling with gay alcoholics can be as rewarding as any other type of counseling.

---

[2]"Coming out" is a three-part process. (1) Acknowledging one's homosexuality to oneself. (2) Revealing oneself as a homosexual to other homosexuals. (3) Declaring one's homosexuality to everyone and anyone. It is the third part of the process that is referred to here. The problems of homosexuals in each part are addressed by Hodges and Hutter (1977, p. 13). Don Clark (1977, pp. 109-147) discusses the problems faced by the family.

Alcoholics Anonymous

Much of this paper has dwelled on the use and role of AA. I frequently attend AA meetings in order to understand further the program and to be able to discuss it with my patients. Because AA groups vary, it also helps to know those meetings where a newly sober person will feel more comfortable. In order to attend a closed gay AA group, I presented a request to the group's business meeting explaining my counseling work with gay alcoholics and my desire to write this paper. The consensus of the group was that I could attend at any time. Up until then, no nongay, nonalcoholic had been allowed at that gay AA meeting. The meetings are very similar to those of other AA groups, except that at gay AA the pronouns do not have to be changed in describing a lover. There is also more freedom to talk about problems, about cruising, coming out, and relationships. The group was helpful, friendly, and willing to answer questions. I learned more about the problems of the gay alcoholic from this source than any other. There were two additional benefits. First was the contact with people who had achieved sobriety only through AA or gay AA but who had never become part of the treatment systems; second was the opportunity to talk with former patients who were still progressing well.

Summary

In summary, a list of recommendations for working with gay alcoholics is offered.

1. Look at your own prejudices. If you are not comfortable in treating a homosexual alcoholic, don't. Come to grips with your own sexuality and know why you are uncomfortable (Williams, Note 2).
2. If you make a referral, make sure not only of the quality of care being offered but also of the person's/agency's ability to accept and work with homosexual alcoholics.
3. Learn the language. Recognize the importance of body language. A firm handshake, relaxed posture, and reassuring physical contact will also express your concern and acceptance (Felman & Morrison, 1977).
4. Be sensitive to laws and their enforcement in your area as regards alcoholism and homosexuality. If great discrepancies exist between the law, institutional policies, hiring practices and their enforcement in your area, you may want to check with a knowledgeable attorney.
5. Develop a knowledge of the medical problems encountered by homosexuals and a referral source of physicians who are willing to treat them and with whom your client can be honest. This is especially important in the area of sexually transmitted diseases (Felman & Morrison, 1977).
6. Be sensitive to the varied life-styles and socioeconomic groups from

which your clients may come, especially those that are different from your own. If you do not understand something, ask. It will strengthen your relationship with your client to show him or her that you care enough to want to know more.

7. Know resources. Get to know gay book stores, gay organizations, gay AA, gay counseling services, and the local gay switchboard or hotline. You will need support systems in a nonalcoholic environment for the gay alcohol abuser. They may also be willing to act as a sounding board for your ideas. This may be especially important if you are the only one in an agency treating homosexuals and you have begun to think you are working in a vacuum. You will then become part of the grapevine which is a major source of communication for the gay and AA communities.

8. Know the literature and use it selectively with clients.

9. Go to gay AA meetings as well as to nongay ones. Know the differences. Try to go with someone who can introduce you to people. Once you have told the members why you are there, most will talk freely. Your clients will feel that you can better understand their AA experiences.

10. Look for common denominators as well as differences. After time, experience, and reading, you will begin to realize that people are not as different as they appear on the surface. If you are neither gay nor a recovering alcoholic, this need not be a hindrance to your ability to provide effective treatment (Loewenstein, 1980).

11. Alcoholics, gay or straight, can be helped to achieve sobriety. The counselor's sense of hope and confidence can be healthfully contagious.

REFERENCE NOTES

1. Olshan, A., Co-owner, Giovanni's Room, Philadelphia, PA. Personal communications, December 8, 1977; March 10, 1980.

2. Williams, K. Overview of sexual problems in alcoholism. Workshop on Sexual Counseling for Persons with Alcoholism, Pittsburgh, PA, January 22-23, 1976.

REFERENCES

Alcoholics Anonymous. *Do you think you're different?* New York: Alcoholics Anonymous World Services, 1976.

American Medical Association. *Manual on alcoholism.* Chicago: American Medical Association, 1977.

Bell, A. P. The homosexual as patient. In M. Weinberg (Ed.), *Sex research: Studies from the Kinsey Institute.* New York: Oxford University Press, 1976.

Clark, D. *Loving someone gay.* Millbrae, CA: Celestial Arts, 1977.

Felman, Y., & Morrison, J. Examining the homosexual male for sexually transmitted disease. *Journal of the American Medical Association*, 1977, 238(19), 246-277.

Hodges, A., & Hutter, D. *With downcast gays: Aspects of homosexual self-oppression.* Toronto: Pink Triangle Press, 1977.

Loewenstein, S. F. Understanding lesbian women. *Social Casework,* 1980, *61*(1), 29-38.

Michael, J. *The gay drinking problem.* Minneapolis: CompCare, 1976.

Michael, J. *Sober, clean, and gay.* Minneapolis: CompCare, 1977.

Richmond, M. *Social diagnosis.* New York: Russell Sage Foundation, 1917.

Snyder, V. Cognitive approaches in the treatment of alcoholism. *Social Casework,* 1975, *56*(8), 480-485.

SPECIFIC APPROACHES AND TECHNIQUES IN THE TREATMENT OF GAY MALE ALCOHOL ABUSERS

Tom Mills Smith, MD

ABSTRACT. An extended discussion of specific therapeutic approaches and techniques with homosexual male alcohol abusers, including dealing with low self-esteem, sober sex, getting high, getting "far out" sexually, double lives, second rate relationships, social bonding, and aging. In this paper, the bias of treatment approaches is toward individualized, interpersonal, holistic eclecticism: a combination of responsibility building therapy, awareness therapy, medical and neurophysiological approaches, strategic therapy, utilization of altered states of consciousness, and attitudinal change therapy.

Available statistics suggest that approximately one-third of homosexual male adults in cosmopolitan areas are alcohol abusers, while one in 10 is the estimate for alcohol abusers in the population at large. This alarming degree of alcoholism in the gay community calls for increased knowledge and resources, utilizing both gay and mixed gay/nongay agencies. This paper will discuss some of the knowledge acquired over the past 10 years by specific services developed to help the gay male alcoholic help himself.

General Considerations

The homosexualities are not pathological entities requiring treatment. Nevertheless, among homosexuals, as among all other people, are individuals who seek treatment for the full range of mental and emotional problems. Gay male clients often require specialized treatment techniques and approaches because of: (1) their particular experiences in life, (2) the unique aspects of the subculture, (3) the individual diversity within this subculture, and (4) frequently encountered attitudes that are different from mainstream social thought and values.

In responding to a particular mental symptom presented by a gay client, the therapist utilizes a "bifocal approach." In one view, the therapist sees the

Dr. Smith is Director of the Alcoholism Evaluation and Treatment Center, San Francisco Medical Center, Department of Public Health, City and County of San Francisco.

53

symptom as unrelated to the homosexuality and focuses treatment as with any other client. In the other view, the therapist sees the symptom as being highly related to the homosexuality and focuses treatment accordingly. The two views are simultaneous. One example is a gay male client who presents in therapy a complaint of unwanted obesity. The one focus would be to approach the client with the usual combination of information, behavior scheduling and contracting, suggestive therapy, support, and occasional insight. During treatment the client may present elaborate defensive excuses: for example, there are no other gays in his Weight Watchers group, his mother forced him to eat, or the therapist doesn't understand his homosexuality. In this case, the client's homosexuality is confronted as a defense against positive change. Simultaneously, the obesity is placed in the context of his gay experiences: for example, his obesity may be a social screen for his homosexuality (reason for not dating women), a defense against intimacy with men (conflicts and disillusionment about homosexual intimacy), a method of appearing younger, and so on.

In many clinical cases, homosexuality is simultaneously seen as an integral part of the problem, and hence of the treatment plan, and also as a grand smoke screen, clouding more basic problems or other anxieties about change. The therapist should explore not only the relationship of the symptom to the client's current life, but also the role that gayness has played in the earlier formation of the symptom. *The therapist must be aware of the usual experiences of the gay child, the gay adolescent, and the gay adult.*

Another major approach in responding to gay males requesting treatment is to enhance awareness of the political and social stresses in his past and in his current life situation and to explore methods of dealing with these stresses. The approach can be closely related to the bifocal approach. Many symptoms in gay males (low self-esteem, paranoia, impotence, shyness, denial, rigidity) are directly related to subtle and gross social oppression and a chronic feeling of impotence in dealing with this unremitting pressure. Group therapy, including consciousness-raising activities and exercises, assertiveness training, and anger and body work, is especially important in this approach. Many chronically depressed, bored, or frustrated gay males make spectacular transformations of their lives in such groups. This phenomenon—this ripeness for self-exploration, self-awareness, and self-assertion—is not only seen in the highly organized "movement" groups, such as *est* or the *Advocate Experience*, but can be just as powerfully felt in grass roots classes, social groups, recreational groups, and less organized activities.

Here the therapist's role is to encourage a change from a passive, victim-restrictive stance to an active, creator-constructive stance. The therapist should not overly interpret the gay male client's nonaggressiveness as passivity, however. Gay males in groups are remarkably congenial. Few physical or verbal fights take place in gay male bars or baths. In group therapy, gay men typically show a high level of mutuality, sharing, and concern.[1] This strong need for positive bonding is an important building block in the therapy of these individuals. Repeated experience shows that if gay men give themselves permission to be open and intimate and develop a minimum of techniques for dealing with rejection and focusing their attention, long held patterns of shyness, reclusiveness, inhibition, and bitterness can be quickly dispelled.

Another general approach for the therapist is to be keenly aware of the individuality of the gay male client. Whereas many gay men move into the gay subculture and adopt its social customs *in toto*, many others do not. Since gay men have few gay role models in their formative years, they develop the full human spectrum of attitudes, feelings, and behaviors. Some gays have high levels of awareness, consciousness, and social liberation while others are highly bigoted, puritanical, and prudish. Many gay men, otherwise sexually active, are negativistic about masturbation, tenderness, or enduring sexual relationships. Many gay men are concerned about being assimilated into the social restrictiveness of a "gay mold," while others desire the freedom to live a "gay life-style." Some wish to explore bisexual, heterosexual, or asexual alternatives. Exercises exploring how the person would like to be can be coupled with information about the variety, the individuality, and the obtainable satisfactions of a gay life-style.

Sex is as important to the gay male as it is to most people. Clinically, sexual behavior should not be overemphasized or overlooked. In exploring gay male sexuality, a familiarity with the varieties of sexual practices and the specific customs of gay male social and sexual settings (such as bars, baths, beaches, and social groups) is helpful to the therapist's understanding the client, implementing goal attainment, and designing assignments and exercises.

Mental health counselors hold many traditional myths concerning gay males. These myths contain a modicum of truth for some, but by no means all individuals and a great deal of unsubstantiated information. Most of these myths are counterproductive in positive change therapy since they are based on assumptions that all gay males are identical, are fixated at regressive levels, and can never achieve a "whole" and satisfactory life. Examples of these myths are: gay males are hysterical and dramatic, especially in dealing with conflict; gay male sex is compulsively driven sex; the treatment objective is a dyadic, long-term relationship; gay males are basically narcissistic; gay sex is basically masturbation; gay males are immature (fixated at pre-Oedipal stages, fixated at adolescence, manifesting the Peter Pan syndrome); gay men are totally sexually liberated; "something" will always be missing, in comparison with

---

[1]In our experience, this is in marked contrast with therapy groups composed of male heterosexual alcoholics. Members of such groups do not at all easily share emotions and self-concepts and often do not exhibit mutual concern or physical closeness (Editors' note).

heterosexuality; gay intimate relationships cannot last and cannot mature; gays are "sad young men"; casual sex is empty sex; gay men are psychotic; gay men cannot obtain relatedness; and so on. *The gay male client also believes many of these myths.* Therapists need to examine their own conceptions of these myths and to be aware of how negative attitudes may interfere with positive change.

There are many important areas of counseling the gay male client—notably, racism, ageism, unrealistic "ideal beauty" standards, parenting, effeminacy, medical aspects, male-female relationships, spirituality, coupling, and group living—that cannot be discussed in the limits of this paper. Therapists should be aware, however, that some or all of these areas may be relevant to treatment of the individual gay male alcoholic.

Specific Approaches and Techniques

The discussion will now focus on frequently encountered aspects of treating gay male alcohol abusers. Case illustrations have been disguised to insure confidentiality.

Bifocal Approach

Being gay has often been used by alcohol abusers as an excuse to continue drinking, to solicit sympathy from friends and counselors, to ward off the anxiety of change, and to keep the counselor at a distance. Alcoholism counselors take a dim view of excuse making of any sort, yet alcoholics can be exceedingly clever in inventing prolific excuses to block change. One gay alcoholic boasted that he had maneuvered heterosexual staff members in several rehabilitation programs into not being able to help because he convinced them that they did not understand his homosexuality. He managed to obtain private rooms in residential treatment agencies and thus was undetected in continued drinking. Homosexuality can be used to play "pity me" as well as "you don't understand" and can be made to sound like an order of a mysterious rite, which it is not. Gay male alcoholics may need confrontation and setting of limits just as much as their nongay counterparts.

Nevertheless, the other part of the bifocal approach is that gayness and alcoholism may be strongly related. In most parts of the country, bars continue to be a major, if not the only, place for gay males to socialize. For many men, alcohol becomes associated with having fun, letting down the socially "correct" stance, and obtaining physical and sexual intimacy. Alcohol is used to reduce the tension of oppression and negative feelings about being gay and about being an alcoholic.

Many gay male alcoholics have not fully accepted their gay experience. They may treasure homosexual desires and find homosexual acts to be necessary, but they do not accept this aspect of their lives. A 50-year-old alcoholic priest (on leave) described episodic periods of guilt starting in pubescence. His mother had died at the time, and he was sent to an orphanage. His guilt increased when he found masturbation and homoerotic fantasies to be "out of control." Alcohol use, starting at age 20, seemed to provide temporary periods of alleviation from his chronically unhappy life. At age 40 he began a series of furtive homosexual experiences with hustlers. He described himself as "obese and ugly" and that "no one would want to touch" him. And no one did. Treatment efforts focused on the childhood depression and his chronic self-punishing behavior and on "here and now" changes that he could make. He developed a list of goals that included attending AA meetings and gay awareness groups, running exercises, and taking a cooking class. He became more focused by writing in a diary and regained an almost lost sense of humor. In his situation, homosexuality, negative feelings, and alcoholism were all thoroughly blended into a black glob that he mistook for his inner self. A key phrase in his treatment was "how much longer will you cling to unhappiness?"

Gay alcoholics often use the phrase "You don't understand." One response would be to say, "You are right, there is much that I don't understand about you. What is it that you would like for me to know?" This resistance utilization is a form of psychological jujitsu where the therapist flows with the energy of the resistance. If gayness continues to be used as a barrier to positive change, then referral to an openly gay counselor would be appropriate. Gayness is rarely used as an "excuse" in a gay alcoholism agency.

Low Self-Esteem

Low self-esteem is frequently an evident symptom in both alcoholics and gay males. Society judges both conditions to be sick, bad, and criminal. In chronic toxic quantities, alcohol greatly interferes with cognition, limiting the individual's grasp of the world, and causes feeling states to become less controlled. The alcoholic begins to perceive the world as a tremendous struggle, and he feels physically ill and depressed.[2] He devalues and blames himself, and he is often angry at himself. Depending upon his personality and experience, he may downgrade everyone else. Negative feelings about his gay experiences become intensified. A satisfactory earlier homosexual adjustment may come into question as do most situations in his life. Even the best of times are viewed negatively.

---

[2]The biological aspects of alcoholism are often given lip service in treatment efforts. Recent radiographic and neuropsychological studies confirm a marked degree of cognitive impairment in chronic alcoholics which, along with persistent physiological disturbances, remains with the individual for a protracted time in the recovery phase. While demeaning "doctor-patient" roles should be avoided, therapy ought to include a labelling of psychological symptoms as related to brain cell dysfunction, a gradual increase of responsibility-taking as organicity subsides, nutritional supplementation, mental stimulation, socialization, and other efforts that relate to brain healing.

A highly successful, 34-year-old businessman entered treatment stating he was not an alcoholic but was very unhappy. He had the Midas touch by day and eight martinis by six o'clock in the evening. In his lovely home he would cry about his lack of friends, his excruciating shyness when sober, his impotence, and his frequent social *faux pas* (actually unsolicited, riotous outbursts). He felt he was ugly because of his baldness. A moment-by-moment exposition of his habits revealed that he actually planned to go out each evening but decided not to after the first drink. In covert rehearsal he fantasized meeting and talking to people. He started receiving weekly body massages. Several months later, during a period of increased socialization, he explored his relationship to his success-oriented, hard-driving father, who had died and disinherited him "because of his homosexuality." This case illustrates the tremendous energy that is often bound down by negative feelings and low self-esteem. The client had a fierce sense of pride and was not about to be told what to do. He was only reluctantly willing to work towards sobriety and happiness.

Some gay male alcoholics with low self-esteem are ripe for intimacy and openness. They are much more readily "lovable" than they give themselves credit for being. Referral to AA and awareness groups often yields dramatic changes and increased self-esteem. Some gay male alcoholics, though, have developed abrasive personalities, clinically indicating a need for character change. As a result of long periods of drinking, they have become unreliable, sarcastic (and sorry later), and embarrassing to themselves and others. In the "rude," bitter gay alcoholic, there is a very low opinion of the identification self and the interpersonal self. Therapy would be directed to anger work, symptom prescription, and perhaps intensive group psychotherapy while maintaining a positive, stable and supportive, dyadic counseling relationship. The motivation to change these abrasive interactions must come from the client. His strengths can be rewarded and separated from negative traits. For example, caustically "bitchy" remarks can be separated into components of wishing to entertain and wishing to hurt others. In written or psychodrama exercises, he can rehearse changing verbal "jabs" into enjoyable laughter.

Self-esteem in gay males is often highly related to body image. When the negativity of alcoholism is added, the person judges himself unattractive. While chronic alcoholism does produce unattractiveness, physical attractiveness can return with abstinence. Skin care; facial, dental, and bodily hygiene; physical fitness exercises; and relaxation exercises can often increase self-esteem and a sense of well-being. Feeling well results in looking well: attractiveness is only partially contingent on physical features and has more to do with mood, health, and personality. Recovering gay alcoholics can be supported in changes of attitude about their appearance that result in increased attractiveness.

Body image is also related to sexual functioning in the gay male. Attitudes towards penis size can have direct effects upon self-esteem and sexual potency. Actually, fears of rejection because of small or variant genitals are usually a smoke screen signaling low self-esteem related to bad "feelings" about gayness and alcoholism. The "worried" individual may develop ways of keeping others away from his genitals during sex. In therapy, which includes giving information about penis sizes, information about "sexual guarding," self-pleasuring exercises, conjoint sexual exercises, affirmation, art therapy with clay, and so forth, the focus is on changing attitudes towards full satisfaction with one's genitals.

Individuals may have similar self-disowning attitudes about other parts of their bodies. This body part rejection may appear trivial and immature, yet to the individual caught up in "ideal beauty" oppression, which may equal the societal oppression of gay people, these attitudes can be central in producing despair, with resulting alcoholism.

Sober Sex

The most frequently seen sexual problems of the gay male alcoholic are decreased sexual desire, decreased sexual feelings, and diminished erections. To this list of problems can be added sexual compulsiveness and lack of experience of satisfactory sex in a drug-free state—that is, "sober sex." Alcohol abuse affects sexual functioning by disturbing hormonal balance, damaging nerves, and increasing fears and worries about sex. Many of these problems improve dramatically with a period of abstinence alone, sexual desire usually returning first, then full erectile and ejaculatory potentials, and finally full sexual feelings. Standard sex therapy techniques can expedite the return to satisfactory sex.

Many alcoholic males are uncomfortable with sex in a sober state of mind. Surprisingly, some sexual athletes are highly embarrassed about sober sex and sexual discussions. One example is a person having wild drunken sex with an individual one night and not speaking to that person the next day, or even 10 minutes later. This also occurs in sober sex and is related to overcompartmentalization of different personality states (the sexual self is not fully accepted by the executive self) with "distancing" mechanisms to block a continuation of the intense sexual relationship. This compartmentalization increases in alcohol abusers, who tend to partition sober and inebriated states and behavior. (Notice the denial inherent in the phrase, "Boy, was I drunk last night!") Blackouts, although caused by different mechanisms (failure of memory imprinting and dissociation), can add to strong separation of the "drunk" sexual self from the "sober" executive self. The latter is often overtly judgmental of the former.

The alcoholic may need to take small steps in learning the great enjoyment of sober sex and to avoid increasing his frustration by adopting a goal of running out and immediately finding a "Mr. Right" with whom to have a mutually rewarding, intensely sexual relationship. Successful completion of self-pleasuring exercises can be followed by nonorgasmic-oriented sex with others. The client's sexual preferences and habits must be kept in mind in coplanning the appropriate progression of sexual exercises.

For example, a 32-year-old bricklayer, sober for six months, complained of retarded ejaculation and diminished sexual feelings in his genitals. He was sexually active, with three visits each week to a partitioned "back room." He enjoyed being the active partner in fellatio; but wished for reciprocation and "bedroom sex." He stated that he had little feeling in his penis, even with masturbation. Using various self-pleasuring and fantasy exercises, he regained full sexual feelings in his genitals and the ability to ejaculate. Upon describing his behavior when he was the receiver of fellatio, he noted that he was very inactive. ("I just stand there.") He was encouraged to send nonverbal messages to his partner about satisfaction received. With time, he learned to be highly communicative with his partners and experienced pleasurable organsms. Partners began to comment favorably on his lovemaking, and he received offers to go to their homes. While encouragement of "back room" sex was very compatible with the desires and goals of this client, the same assignment would be totally rejected by many other clients and would be totally inappropriate. The therapist must go at the client's pace and prescribe exercises that fit the individual.

Sexual compulsiveness is not the same as high sexual frequency or so-called "casual" sex. Many gay men find frequent "casual" sex to be highly satisfactory, often filled with intense, intimate exchanges, including intimate conversation and shared altered states of consciousness, albeit of short duration. These sexual encounters can be highly "objectified" and masturbatory or they can contain a meaningful intense emotional exchange. The value system of the client must be given importance since casual sexual relationships are unjustly discriminated against through cultural notions. Quite often the client does not wish to give up his behavior but rather wants enrichment and satisfaction, while recognizing that his values are contrary to society's emphasis on monogamy and stability.

Sexual compulsiveness, on the other hand, is "driven" behavior usually without any lasting satisfaction.[3] Sexual compulsiveness can be masturbating nine times a day or visiting the "bookstore" every day, though these acts can also be "nonpathological." Exploiting paradoxical intention is effective in changing unwanted sexual compulsions. A 39-year-old artist, sober six months, went to bars several times a day to make sexual contacts. He drank only mineral water but was afraid that he would start drinking alcohol again. He felt driven to have sex several times a day. This compulsion had increased over

---

[3]Many chronic alcoholics have compulsive personalities and can become compulsive in many different aspects of their lives (sex, eating, tobacco smoking, work). The therapist must remember, however, that compulsiveness also serves as a way of organizing, structuring, and obtaining success in one's life.

the preceding three months. He was encouraged to have a "sexual marathon," keeping exact records on how many sexual encounters he had in a day. He was advised to rest for two days prior to the marathon and to get his chores and business affairs in order so that he could spend all his time in bed. He participated in the sexual marathon for four days and settled down with the fourteenth person. Several months later he reported happiness in his new relationship, with infrequent yet pleasurable, short-term sex "on the side." This case illustrates the successful planning of paradoxical intention and symptom prescription, utilizing several interrelated factors: awareness, symptom performed under instruction, symptom performed with permission, symptom controlled rather than out of control, and so forth.

After years of conditioning himself to sexual experiences only when intoxicated, the alcoholic may become anesthetized to sensitive sexual communication (synchronous flow) and may increasingly focus on unilateral sex: that is, pleasuring only himself or only his partner. Treatment emphasis in these situations is toward sensual awareness, attention focusing alternating between analytical thinking and feeling state "thinking," changing attitudes from unilateral sex to synchronous flow, learning sexual communication, "getting into" the sex act, and relaxing and being open with others. (The reader is referred to Silverstein & White, 1977, for further information.)

Getting High

Evidence shows that "being high" is an altered state of consciousness. Most alcoholics do not understand that the brain has an ability to get "high" naturally, without psychotropic substances, and that alcohol only speeds up this natural process (Weil, 1973). Getting high naturally can be a purely intuitive event, yet several factors will increase the likelihood of attaining peaks of altered consciousness: (1) knowing about altered states, (2) giving oneself permission to "let go," (3) selecting a conducive environment, (4) relaxing, (5) concentrating, (6) adopting a noncritical stance, (7) breathing exercises, and (8) rhythms (music, dance, etc.). Giving information about altered consciousness is not enough. The alcoholic is not convinced that he can have a sober "high" until he has actually experienced these altered states without drugs. Hundreds of useful exercises that stimulate natural "highs" are described in books on Awareness Therapy, Neo-Reichian body work, various meditation techniques, dance and theater games therapy, Tantra practices, breathing therapies, and so on. These exercises run the gamut from rituals and disciplines to everyday momentary practices.

Many gay men retain anxiety about "getting high," associating altered states of consciousness with (1) "living in fantasy," (2) years of sickness and compulsiveness, (3) escapism, (4) failure and demoralization, and (5) fear. What is not fully recognized is that "high" states can increase the satisfaction of interpersonal exchanges and perceptions of the environment. An exploration of fears of "getting high" and methods for handling these fears are usually helpful for recovering alcoholics who do not wish to learn the techniques of natural highs.

Because alcoholics often compartmentalize behavior into behavior while inebriated and behavior while sober, personal strengths and desired behavior, such as having fun and being spontaneous, may be delegated to the inebriated state (for example, the alcoholic who is the life of the party when drunk and painfully shy when sober). Using altered states of consciousness exercises without chemicals, the recovering alcoholic can experience these behaviors and continue to experience them in everyday life. An example is a 42-year-old, chronically depressed and staid professor with one year of sobriety who became very playful in group hypnosis sessions. He gradually became more spontaneous and playful in his everyday life. Fears of being discovered as gay and as alcoholic had combined to produce a restricted personality. Warm, supportive friends helped him release his "pent-up, natural, free child."

Getting "Far Out" Sexually

Getting "far out" sexually indicates sexual explorations beyond "traditional" practices. "Far out" designates an attitude rather than specific sexual acts: for example, fellatio may be "far out" to some individuals while others would consider fellatio a basic technique and "watersports" to be "far out." Most types of "kinky" sex have origins in and are on a continuum with "traditional" sexual practices. For example, "bondage" is akin to being hugged and "humiliation" is akin to "dirty" pillow talk. Viewing sexual activities on a spectrum helps a client sort out which parts of the behavior are desired and which are unwanted.

Getting "far out" sexually usually has a high intensity quality, a high degree of sensuality, and a high level of interpersonal exchange. Sometimes, but certainly not usually, getting "far out" sexually includes elements of breaking taboos, flirting with danger, or eroticizing nonerotic activities. Danger, fear, and pain that signals tissue damage have all been eroticized, possibly because of the high intensity levels inherent in these emotions.

Gay alcoholic men may have excessive guilt concerning past sexual activities —they have not been able to integrate the "high" or "far-outness" of these experiences into their sober lives. They might have placed themselves in dangerous or embarrassing situations, become disgusted or bored during the sex act, and continued to drink to obliterate the memories. Many alcoholics do not wish to remember or explore these negatively held, past experiences. Therapy would be aimed not at exploration, but rather toward a progression of exercises to regain sexual joys.

On the other hand, many of these negatively held experiences "happened" without much conscious thought or discussion with others. These acts are often sequestered into secrecy and silence. Open discussion can help sort out which parts of these experiences were beneficial and would like to be retained and which parts are loathsome and need to be discarded. The therapist must here again remain attuned to the client's value system. Many people value and make conscious decisions to retain their "kinky" sex practices.

Some "far out" sex acts may have become obsessive and compulsive. The person constantly thinks about these acts and feels driven to perform them. He may drink to complete the compulsion. As mentioned before, compulsive sexual behavior fails to give satisfaction beyond the momentary experience. The individual might even become bored during the sex act. ("What am I doing here?") The individual often tries to control the compulsion by resolving to quit the behavior, only to return on impulse and feel even greater guilt and loss of control. Treatment would focus on permitting continuation of the sex acts, but with increased sensuality, intimacy, and sharing.

Double Lives

Most people develop different ways of behaving in different environments, and this versatility, when creative rather than regressive, is labelled as a strength. Problems arise when the personality states are too dissociated, when amnesia develops between the states, or when areas of the personality are overly restricted (illustrated, for example, by the loss of spontaneity in public by some gay people). Mechanisms of maintaining secrecy of the hidden self can occur in both alcoholics and in gay males, and the individual may become overly protective lest anyone find out about his alcoholism or about his gayness. Morbid defenses may include lying, minimal communication, evasiveness, shyness, and various degrees of paranoia.

A 58-year-old electrician with three years of sobriety did not reveal homosexual interests until after eight months of therapy. He had earlier fabricated a story of a previous wife and daughter. Over the years he had become reclusive and secretive. Therapy progressed slowly with encouragement for him to socialize. He became uncomfortable in his therapy group and at AA meetings and would blame various members for not understanding him, listing their faults. He stated that he was lying to the group and was revealing little about himself. Therapy included active listening exercises, role reversal in psychodrama, anger exploration, reframing, symptom prescription of lying, and so on. Several months later he had developed three close friends.

Discomfort in either the sober or "straight acting" states can lead to increasing withdrawal from society into a cloistered, secretive world. Some gay male alcoholics begin to spend increasing amounts of time drunk and exclusively in the "gay world." They may develop a vivid fantasy life that begins to be more real than their sober life. A 30-year-old opera singer, sober for two months, stated that he lived in a world of fantasy where he was exceedingly rich and famous. His "real life" relationships were with older "patrons." He stated that he chose drunkenness because he could continue to dream and not bother with his feelings of being "controlled" and being "dirty." He magically visualized himself singing at the Met without any realistic plans as to how his singing career could progress. With several months of sobriety, he decided to seek out vocational nurse's training and to join a community chorus. He went through a period of mourning over the loss of his fantasy life.

Double lives might include "secret" sex lives that are only practiced during drunken states, are a source of extreme guilt, and are not shared with anyone, including gay friends. A 40-year-old clerk decided that he was "no longer in the market" as far as sex and intimacy were concerned. While drunk he would cross-dress and fantasize life into inanimate objects. Not until several years after sobriety could he talk about these experiences.

Some alcoholics have not fully "come out" to themselves. They report that their drinking helps to deny their homoerotic thoughts and actions. These individuals need information and support, especially group support. A 32-year-old accountant had been celibate until age 31. He had a satisfactory homosexual experience while on vacation, then drank for two months afterwards. He repeated these homosexual encounters followed by binge drinking several times over the following nine months. He questioned whether he was "gay or straight." Therapy focused on abstinence, sexual information, exploration of his sexual feelings and desires, and sexual awareness exercises. He decided to visit gay and bisexual therapy groups, nongay and gay AA groups. Several months later he decided that he wanted to pursue sober gay experiences.

The therapy of double lives, similar to the treatment of dissociative states (multiple personalities), is towards integration of the different personality states into a more open, more aware, and more flexible personality.

Second Rate Relationships

Gay relationships are generally viewed as second rate: "Two men can never achieve a full, stable, satisfactory, growth producing relationship." First rate gay male relationships, which are intimate, mutually sharing, and of equal partners, are not well publicized. Inebriated gay males are perhaps more prone to experience second rate relationships where one person is seen as more highly valued than the other, with the alcoholic taking the "low man" position. Once a relationship is "labelled" second rate, the partners will find it difficult to change into a pairing of equals. Subtle rejection of each other usually cannot be overcome. For example, an alcoholic couple had barely survived years of berating each other. One demeaned the other's obesity, yet kept the kitchen full of pasta and beer. The trim partner was derided about his acne and his use of cosmetics. Both individuals harbored years of resentment against the other. Upon obtaining sobriety, the couple decided to terminate the relationship, despite AA, couples therapy, and individual psychotherapy.

The labelling of a relationship as second rate is often used as a defense against intimacy, an excuse for not being involved, a paradoxical protection of self-esteem, and as a control of others. Second rate relationship labelling may become habitual, whereby all relationships are seen by the individual as second rate, and may be an automatic function of social labels (e.g., "all black-white couples are of the haves and have-nots" or "all older-younger relationships are exploitive"). Second rate labelling may also be related to some form of sado-masochism.

The basic issues for gay male alcoholics in the problem of relationship labelling are best countered with continued sobriety, increased awareness, increased self-esteem, increased communication skill attainment, and a change in attitudes of viewing others.

Social Bonding

Many gay men have strong desires to form close friendship networks. Gay couples and single gay men may join to form dinner party groups, bridge clubs, celebrations, political groups, self-help groups, and so on. Gay friends may live in close proximity, sometimes in the same apartment building or in communal houses. Many gay men recreate a sense of family and community. These groups often include lesbians and heterosexual men and women. Viewing the gay man as isolated and lonely is not very accurate; however, the view of the drinking alcoholic as alienated is often quite accurate. Steiner (1971) describes how alcoholics become frustrated in needing interpersonal closeness and yet alienating others at the same time.

Alcohol abuse may affect gay men's social bonding patterns in many different ways. Gay men may start drinking as a method of dealing with the primary family. Sometimes excessive drinking is used as a way of separating from or of coping with overly involved and overly dependent parents. A 49-year-old janitor, sober six months, reported that his mother, in whose house he rented a room, had recently become overbearing. He was attending AA ("Sixty meetings in sixty days") and was spending more time away from home than he had ever managed before. For a while he had become less involved with his mother. She increased her nagging about his household chores. Therapy sessions were arranged to take place in his room so that his mother could overhear that she was loved and would not be abandoned. Several weeks later she started attending church services, which she had forsaken after the death of her husband 45 years before.

Some recovering alcoholics state that they have not had any friends in years and find group activities, including AA meetings, to be overwhelming. The therapist can explore the client's fantasies about how he would like to be socially. During a relaxation exercise the client can be encouraged to recall past social situations in which he related comfortably, often in adolescence or childhood. Nearly all individuals have had periods of open communication with school friends, siblings, or cousins, and new social skills can be added in a slow progression to those previously acquired.

A 40-year-old night shift nurse, sober for two years, stated that he had always been a loner and was feeling especially lonely over the past six months. A woman friend, his nursing supervisor, had died two months prior to the onset of his intense lonely feelings. He did not wish to talk about his platonic relationship with her. He insisted that he had never been close to anyone, yet he recalled relationships with a female cousin at age seven and a close male schoolmate in junior high school. He remembered sharing secrets and jokes. He had forgotten about this playful aspect of himself. He was reluctant to try a return to AA after he had attended two "straight" meetings during detoxification. His first assignment was to go to several meetings, to arrive as the meeting began, to sit near the door, and to stay for a brief period of time. At the next session he reported that he had attended two AA meetings and that he had stayed for the entire meeting. He was encouraged to try other meetings. Several weeks later he reported weekly attendance at a gay AA meeting; however, he continued to avoid social contact. He was encouraged to arrive early and to stay a few minutes after the meeting to help put away chairs. Several weeks later he reported talking to several people. He felt his conversation was awkward. In psychodrama he practiced meeting people and developed conversational topics of general interest. Three weeks later he reported that he had established several friendships and that he was giving a small dinner party.

Older Gay Male Alcoholics

The commercialized emphasis on youth can put many stresses on the gay male alcoholic. Both gayness and alcoholism are not taken as seriously in the young person as compared to the person in middle or old age. ("It's just a phase he is going through; he'll grow out of it.") The punishment or negative consequences of gayness and alcoholism are seen as occurring in middle or later life. ("It will catch up with him sooner or later.") Many myths abound about older gay men: they will grow old, lonely, and alone; gay men are dirty old men after the age of 40 (or thirty!); older gay men commit suicide or go crazy; older gay men are all old queens or aunties; and on and on. Even though studies of older gay men indicate that these myths are quite unfounded, many gay men believe that life after 40 will indeed be bleak.

This pessimism is accentuated in the gay male alcoholic. He is often confronted with sexual impotence; premature aging of his visible body; multiple illnesses that are associated with alcohol and other drug abuse; and losses of status, friends, and self-esteem. Too often the aging alcoholic erroneously feels that he must pay for his past mistakes and frivolities. Even though he has heard that alcoholism is an illness, he continues to believe that he is to blame. Alcoholism is still treated as a weakness, a sin, and a crime.

The despondency of the gay male alcoholic may intensify protective mechanisms. He may become jaded, impervious to any new delights. He may become defensive in conversation—nothing pleases him, nothing can influence him to compromise and to share. Previous experiences of being open and impressionable only lead to pain. His wall overprotects him. This defensiveness is usually a result of years of thinking, feeling, and behaving in an inebriated state. Along with sobriety, he can learn new subtle ways of communicating with openness and warmth.

The despondency of the gay male alcoholic may result in morbid dependency. A 65-year-old auto mechanic, sober for one year, had frequent periods of depression. The death of his lover of 15 years had led to several months of almost suicidal drinking, then detoxification. He had taken to AA meetings "like a duck to water." He was active in several groups and on several committees. Yet he felt uneasy around his new friends. He described a change in himself over the past three years from being a strong, self-sufficient individualist to being clinging and pleasantly overbearing. He could not do enough for others. He called all his friends frequently but noted that he received few calls. He was not unhappy with his new life, but realistically he wanted to return to being self-sufficient. He was afraid of becoming attached to just one person, yet he was afraid that he would become alone and lonely. He was encouraged to continue his active role as a helper and to explore areas in the group in which he could assume responsibility. He was also encouraged to get a sponsor several years older than himself. A year later he had entered into a coupled relationship and had continued his social and fellowship activities.

The alcoholism counselor must be aware that the gay subculture is very changeable and has many interrelated subgroups. Several of these distinguishable groups have to do with the decades of this century in which gay men entered into the gay subculture. The subculture of the 1930s is very different from today's subculture. The oppression of the 1950s produced secrecy and denial; the oppression of the 1970s produced militancy and organization. Different decades have produced different "gay sensibilities," different ways of dressing and speaking, different attitudes. Some gay alcoholics have difficulties in being able to deal with these changes of the subculture within the changes of the society at large. Therapy groups with some older individuals in the same age bracket are often helpful in reducing isolation, in providing successful role models, in fostering the sharing of gay "old times," and in supporting members.

In addition to knowledge of the subcultural changes, the therapist must be aware of the different developmental tasks, as described by Erik Erikson, that gay men face in different periods of their lives. Gay men have the same challenges that confront their heterosexual counterparts, and gay men can just as successfully complete these stages. The stage of generativity includes more than parenting, though a sizeable fraction of gay men are fathers. Older recovering gay alcoholics need more information about the joys and strengths that are contained within the second half of life. Often the older gay male will broaden his acceptance of life and of others, abandoning the restrictions of youth that were previously used to bolster his self-esteem.

Conclusion

The specific treatment approach to any problem presented by the gay male alcoholic is to recognize the client as an individual who has particular and unique life experiences. He may be part of the gay subculture and the gay alcoholic subculture. He may hold some attitudes that are different from those of society at large. Knowledge of this subculture, of the various surroundings in which the gay alcoholic lives, and of the varying attitudes within the gay world, is almost essential in aiding the therapist to understand the client and his problems and to formulate an appropriate treatment plan. The therapist must be flexible enough to consider a wide variety of value systems. If the therapist is convinced that the client's outlook is immature, destructive, or restrictive, then the therapist can voice these concerns, stating clearly, however, that these are personally held, biased views.

Even though cessation of alcohol abuse is best accomplished by an abrupt halt of drinking, therapeutic change often begins with subtle, small changes in the problematic behavior. These changes can be initiated by homework assignments that are carried out in the person's everyday life or are rehearsed in psychodrama or in fantasy exercises. A therapeutic advantage exists if the therapist is familiar with the physical appearance and usual social behavior that takes place in gay environments. Another advantage exists in knowledge of the roles played by the gay male alcoholic and how others respond to him.

The therapist should know about the life stages of gay males, how these different stages affect the symptoms of alcoholism, and how alcohol abuse interrelates with behavior during these stages. For example, many gay men develop homoerotic feelings early in life and also feel that they are "different." These feelings of being separate may intensify into paranoia, depression, denial, and so on. Alcohol may be used as a coping mechanism to deal with the anxiety associated with these symptoms. This approach to the gay alcoholic is not ahistorical. The therapist utilizes the client's past in order to understand the formation and perpetuation of behaviors that affect the "here and now." This approach fully utilizes psychodynamics and the effects of interpersonal relationships.

In treating gay male alcoholics, the therapist needs to be aware of the many stresses upon the client that arise from society, from the gay subculture, and from the client's psyche, not only because of gayness, but also because of the alcoholism. Many gay male alcoholics are oppressed in several different ways by assaults on different aspects of their personality and constitution. Since the client often does not describe these pressures, the therapist must be attuned to what the client might be experiencing and must then confirm and affirm these presumptions by discussions with the client.

Society is lessening the multiple oppressions upon gay people, upon men, and upon alcoholics. Many new techniques, often based upon folk wisdom, are now being effectively utilized to facilitate the recovery from alcoholism and to enhance the satisfaction in the lives of gay men.

REFERENCES

Silverstein, C., & White, E. *The joy of gay sex*. New York: Simon and Schuster, 1977.
Steiner, C. *Games alcoholics play*. New York: Grove Press, 1971.
Weil, A. *The natural mind*. Boston: Houghton Mifflin, 1973.

A GAY-IDENTIFIED ALCOHOL
TREATMENT PROGRAM:
A FOLLOW-UP STUDY

Rosanne Driscoll, RN, MEd

ABSTRACT. The Homophile Alcohol Treatment Service (HATS) is an urban Boston out-patient clinic. A survey to assess program effectiveness, reported here, demonstrates that HATS has been able to promote less harmful drinking behaviors in its clients and to educate clients about alcohol-related health hazards. Issues around reaction to gay clients in nongay treatment agencies, accessibility of services, and survey problems in the gay community are discussed with their implications for improving services like HATS.

The Homophile Alcoholism Treatment Service (HATS) is the alcoholism service of Boston's Homophile Community Health Services (HCHS), a mental health outpatient clinic serving homosexual men and women and their families. Depending on circumstances, the identified client could be an individual, couple, or family. Additionally, community-wide services are provided. Services encompass prevention and early identification, treatment and referral, and follow-up, support, and after-care referral. Specific programs at any time might include:

— *Prevention/Intervention.* In-service training on alcoholism to HCHS staff, workshops and conferences for gay organizations on alcoholism and to nongay agencies on the treatment of gays, priority consultation policy with HCHS (as noted below), a drop-in center, an alcohol education and support group.
— *Treatment/Referral.* Individual, couples, and group therapy; referral to detoxification centers or halfway houses previously determined to be helpful to gays. When clients present themselves for HCHS treatment of problems other than alcohol and alcohol seems problematic, agency policy requires a HATS consultation with the client. If alcohol abuse is indicated, treatment for alcoholism is given priority. (This policy adds to

Rosanne Driscoll, a former staff member of the Homophile Alcoholism Treatment Services in Boston, prepared this paper as part of her graduate program at Boston State College. Her current address is 94 Fawndale Road, Roslindale, MA 02131.

71

the number of high denial clients seen by HATS.) Following intake consultation, a treatment plan is developed, and clients contract for specific programs.
— *Follow-up/Support.* Alcoholics Together (AT) and Alcoholics Anonymous (AA) groups for recovering alcoholics, vocational counseling, referral to community agencies.

Other ongoing projects include the opening of services to the deaf and the creation of a halfway house committee attempting to obtain a halfway house for gay men and women.

The program has existed in this basic form since July 1978. Prior to that, beginning in 1975, alcohol services were offered by alcoholism counselors of HCHS without separate name or extended services. (These stages of the program will be referred to as "post-HATS" and "pre-HATS" in later discussions.)

The program serves gay alcoholics in eastern Massachusetts. Little is known for certain about the drinking habits of this population. In 1978, the Boston Gay Health Collective distributed 15,000 questionnaires through gay organizations. Only 1,087 were returned and usable. Don Barrett (Note 1), in an unpublished paper for HATS, analyzed the results of the four questions in this survey which concerned alcohol use. From self-report, 19% of the respondents drank daily. Average daily consumption for this group was 3.4 drinks. Another 22% of the respondents drank 3 to 4 times per week, with average daily consumption of 3.3 drinks. Another 28% drank mainly on weekends with average consumption of 7.1 drinks per weekend. Another 3% reported days or weeks of heavy drinking, 5% did not drink, and another 5% used to drink but no longer did so.

Of the daily drinkers, 47% felt that at some time, at least once, they had had a problem with alcohol such as missing work, driving violations, medical problems or injury, or getting into arguments with friends. The daily average consumption of this subgroup was 4.1 drinks per day. Of the 3 to 4 times a week drinkers, 33% had experienced an alcohol-related problem and their average consumption was 4.1 drinks per drinking day. 26% of the mainly weekend drinkers experienced a problem at some time, and their weekend consumption was reported as 13.6 drinks per weekend.

HATS is based upon the premise that a gay-identified alcoholism service agency can better provide supportive counseling and therapy which focuses on changing the patterns of alcohol consumption in gay men and women. At HATS, we have had many clients who have been in previous treatment with traditional agencies who, while they originally presented themselves as seeking help with difficulties with alcohol or depression, found that the therapist had another agenda: treating the homosexuality. Gay-identified therapists repeatedly find that the fear of confronting this hidden agenda had prevented many gay clients from seeking therapy. Many gay men and women fear "coming out" to the therapist who works in a traditional setting.

Program Evaluation

In evaluating the effectiveness of the HATS program, an attempt was made to address the usual criteria for evaluating intervention outcomes. According to Blane (1977), drinking frequency, including both abstinence and decreased consumption, is the most common criteria for outcome studies. Beyond drinking behavior, the present study is concerned with the effectiveness of the health education offered. Every intake form used by HCHS and HATS has had questions on family health problems of the client. Counselors doing intake pursue noteworthy responses and are particularly aware of the potential health problems complicated by alcohol. It is known, then, that there is at least minimal attention paid to health education in this initial intake. The evaluators were concerned with how effective this teaching is. Client's recollection of having discussed health care was taken to mean that the teaching was effective. Additional parameters of health education evaluation appear in the survey questionnaire reproduced in the Appendix.

The third area of concern is the collection of subjective reports of experiences in nongay traditional treatment and why people chose gay-identified treatment. This information is useful in workshops. The evaluators also wanted feedback for program review on what kinds of programs facilitated or impeded recovery. While questions on these matters are included in the survey, not all the information is included in the present study.

Method

Subjects: All the clients of HATS and the predecessor Alcohol Services of HCHS who had contracted for services and had at least four therapy sessions were taken as subjects. From this group, three subpopulations were acknowledged. Twenty-five were currently active and were called the "current" group. Forty-one had terminated since reorganization and were called the "post-HATS" group. Forty-three had been terminated prior to reorganization in 1978 and were called the pre-HATS group.

Materials: A questionnaire consisting of two pages of closed and open-ended questions was sent to all clients. (See Appendix A.) Sample questions included the following items: How many alcoholic drinks did you have yesterday? Were medical issues addressed during your intake or during your therapy? Why did you come to a gay-identified agency? The questionnaires and self-addressed, stamped envelopes were sufficient for three mailings.

Procedures: At the beginning of 1980, the counseling staff of HATS distributed the questionnaire to their active clients requesting that the clients fill out the questionnaire at home and return it to the office. The questionnaire was mailed to the terminated clients together with a self-addressed, stamped envelope. When replies ceased coming into the office, a second mailing went out to all subjects from whom neither a reply nor an undeliverable questionnaire was received. Similarly, a third mailing was made when replies from the second slowed down. There were so few additional replies from the third mailing that no fourth attempt was made.

Results

The poor return rate—16 active, 21 post-HATS and 6 pre-HATS—was disappointing but not unexpected. Because the pre-HATS returns were so far below 50%, the minimum figure the evaluators would accept, these results were not considered except for demographic and anecdotal information. Notations were made on the questionnaire about treatment dates and time lapsed since termination to facilitate logging.

Demographics: Seventy-nine percent of the clients were male. The average age was 29, with a range from 19 to 53. An overwhelming majority was from Boston City proper, and nearly all were from the Greater Metropolitan Boston area. A rank ordering of towns can be found in Table 1. A rank ordering of referral sources included friends, HCHS/HATS staff, Gay Hotline, Massachusetts Rehabilitation Commission, newspapers, nongay agencies, family, and doctor. (See Table 2.)

Drinking behavior: The HATS program philosophy supported the individual's decision to choose with his counselor either abstinence or controlled social drinking. Consequently, different goals need to be kept in mind while assessing outcomes.

Considering all clients, abstainers and controlled drinkers combined, 94% of the actives (15 of 16 clients) and 81% of the "post-HATS" (17 out of 21 clients) did not drink yesterday. The one drinker in the active group had five drinks. The average consumption for the drinkers in the post-HATS group was 3.25 drinks. In the active group, 69% did not drink "this week." The drinkers in the active group averaged six drinks for the week, and the drinkers in the post-HATS group averaged 30.5 drinks for the week.

Seventy-one percent of those for whom abstinence was a goal (10 of 14) were abstinent during the last three months. These were all clients who had terminated at least four months ago (see Table 3). This figure is remarkably high. Table 4 indicates that 58% of planned abstainers out of treatment at least seven months had refrained from drinking alcohol (7 of 12). This figure is also high. If one wanted to assume most pessimistically that the entire population lost to follow-up had been drinking, the overall program achievement would thereby be reduced by one-half to 35% maintaining controlled drinking

Table 1. Rank Ordering of Towns
of Service by Agency

Boston	25
Cambridge, Somerville, Acton, Quincy	2 each
Newton, Groveland, Middleboro, Watertown, Lynn, Dedham, Waltham, Randolph	1 each

Table 2. Rank Ordering of Referral
Source Where Indicated

Friend	13
HCHS/HATS staff	8
Gay Hotline, Mass. Rehab. Comm., Fenway Gay Clinic	2 each
Gay Community News, Samaritans, Project Place, Clinic Without Walls, Paulist Fathers, Boston Globe, Phoenix, doctor, brother	1 each

and 26% maintaining abstinence. These conservatively derived figures compare with the upper range figure and the median figure reported by Blane (1977) for outcomes of other programs.

To provide another perspective, one could define therapeutic effectiveness as successfully providing a client the opportunity to achieve longer periods of abstinence than he or she could achieve prior to treatment. Tables 5 and 6 show the compared level of abstinence before and after treatment for the active and post-HATS groups respectively, where abstinence was the goal. In the active group where every "after" entry is greater than its paired "before" entry, treatment effectiveness is obvious. For the post-HATS group, a Wilcoxon's t-statistic for the matched pairs, signed ranks test was computed and t (n = 16)

Table 3.   Number of Times Drinking in Last 3 Months
           as a Function. of Time Since Termination
           (By those with abstinence as a goal)

	Months since termination			
	4-6	7-9	10-12	>12
Number of	0	4	0	0
times	0	140	0	0
drinking		0	2	
(by subject)		0		
		0		
		0		
		many		

Table 4.   Number of Times Drinking in Last 6 Months
           as a Function of Time Since Termination
           (By those with abstinence as a goal)

	Months since termination		
	7-9	10-12	>12
Number of	0	4	0
times	400	0	0
drinking	drank	3	
(by subject)	0		
	0		
	0		
	drank		

was 23.5 (p < 0.01). It is therefore concluded that HATS treatment was significantly helpful to the post-HATS group in attaining longer periods of sobriety.

HATS did not have a fixed time duration as part of its protocol. Clients needing more support could be seen longer. When a *t*-test for a difference between two independent means was made (Table 7), comparing number of times drinking in the last three months between post-HATS clients with six or less months of treatment (short term) and seven or more months (long term), the result was $t(19) = 1.24$ (p < 0.1). This indicates that there is a significant difference in outcome between the drinking of those clients who received short term therapy and those who were felt to require more support and got longer treatment contracts. The longer term clients did not do so well. An alternative to outpatient HATS treatment should be found for these more "disabled" clients.

Table 5. Client's Longest Period of
Abstinence Before Treatment and After
Treatment Compared by Subject

	Before Treatment	After Treatment
Weeks of	27	63
abstinence	0	22.5
(by subject)	4.5	20
	9	22.5
	9	18
	0	9
	13.5	22.5
	2	6
	0	54
	0	54
	0	36
	0.5	29.2
mean value	5.5	29.7
std. dev.	8.2	18.4

Table 6. Post-HATS Group Longest
Abstinence Before and After Treatment
Compared by Subject

	Before Treatment	After Treatment
Weeks of	13.5	63
abstinence	4.5	135
(by subject)	0	22.5
	54	31.5
	90	22.5
	0	31.5
	9	54
	0	36
	20	2
	1	45
	13.5	9
	27	81
	2	83.5
	0	3
	0	27
mean value	14.7	42.2
std. dev.	28.6	34.7

Table 7. Post-HATS Group: Number
of Times Drinking in Past 3 Months
Compared by Short and Long Term Clients

	Short Term Clients	Long Term Clients
Number of	0	140
times	0	0
drinking	50	0
(by subject)	90	39
	0	0
	2	12
	0	
	0	
	2	
	0	
	12	
	0	
	0	
	0	
	0	

Health care: The third area of concern was education for health care. Successful intervention can be taken to mean recollection of medical issues being discussed during therapy, making follow-up plans for medical care, or obtaining helpful educational and planning assistance. In the active group, 56% of responders indicated a recall that medical issues were addressed during intake or therapy; 37% made follow-up plans for health care; 50% found the program helpful in coordinating, planning or educating them for medical care. In the post-HATS group, 63% reported recall that medical issues were addressed; 10% made follow-up, and 21% found the program helpful. It is hoped that this difference reflects increased staff awareness and commitment to promoting primary health care.

Treatment patterns: It was helpful to the evaluators to know how "experienced" the clients were in treatment. Fifty percent of the post-HATS group and all but two of the active group were "treatment virgins" before coming to HATS. The 10 post-HATS clients with previous treatment for alcoholism averaged 7.1 previous treatments. (S.D. = 8). After HATS treatment termination, 4 people sought treatment elsewhere, with a mean of 1.25 subsequent contacts.

The increased proportion of "treatment virgins" in the later clientele was attributed to the many outreach and community education programs conducted by the agency. Because of these efforts, potential treatment population members were aware that gay-identified treatment exists and those who had not before sought help are evidently being reached by this exposure. The overwhelming modal response to the question: "Why did you come to a gay-identified agency?" was, "Because I am gay." There were also many responses citing actual or anticipated discrimination in treatment.

Discussion

Demographics: That so few women came to the agency is a matter of concern, and it is evident that the community needs women's services. The addition of more women to the counseling staff seems to have brought more women into the agency. In addition, if someday HATS were able to provide child care, it is likely they would be able to expand services to this population.

Drinking behaviors: Despite heavy reliance on a transient staff of volunteers, practicum students, and work-study students, with only one full-time person, the program has done well. Despite staff changes at the end of academic years when practicum students change over, HATS has demonstrated the ability to provide services at least equal to those elsewhere (compare with Blane's, 1977, results), and td reach a population otherwise serviced poorly. On the other hand, it is unfortunate that HATS has only 25 active clients, if 10% of the metropolitan Boston population is homosexual and if 33% of that group is in trouble with alcohol. Alcoholism services, even if good, are inadequate. Those clients who are recipients of long term therapy by reason of perceived need are cases in point. There are few halfway houses to which HATS can confidently refer clients without fearing they will experience some negative reaction to their homosexuality. At present, there is no gay halfway house, nor is there recourse to legal action in the event discrimination occurs in Massachusetts. Perhaps if such a house existed, clients would reach it at an earlier stage in their illness when treatment would be more easily accomplished.

Health care: Because alcoholics are at risk for many other health problems, it is well that HATS continues to promote early diagnosis and treatment of related health problems in its clients. Health education also has the positive feature of being something one can offer the early treatment drop-out that will still benefit the client. It is disappointing that more HATS clients do not have regular health care providers. Perhaps one way to increase health care concern would be to provide monthly health education seminars to all clients.

Treatment patterns: Considering the anecdotal information together with our survey data showing the percentage of persons new to therapy, it may be assumed that fear of rejection keeps many homosexuals away from traditional services. It is evident that when gay-identified therapy is available, clients will come, and they will come to gay services sooner that they will go to nongay services. The furthest points from which subjects travelled to come to Boston include Groveland, Acton, and Middleboro. It seems grossly paradoxical that in a society so concerned about accessibility of services to the physically challenged and other special population categories, homosexuals are denied readily available services.

Recommendations for further research: Population surveys in the gay community are often difficult. Although it is sometimes necessary to conduct surveys in order to compare data with nongay-identified populations, alternatives for use within the gay population should be found. One possibility would be a repeat of the Barrett study drawn from the Gay Health Collective survey. Since HATS considers primary prevention a major responsibility, changes in the drinking of the community as a whole might reflect the effectiveness of the program. Unobtrusive measures of gay bar drinking and gay recreational drinking would be another possibility. As long as gay alcoholism continues to be a major health hazard, any novel assessment technique which directs services into the community is appropriate.

REFERENCE NOTE

1. Barrett, D. Report on alcohol use and abuse for HATS. Unpublished manuscript, 1979.

REFERENCE

Blane, H. T. Issues in evaluation of alcohol treatment. *Professional Psychology*, November 1977.

APPENDIX
Survey Questionnaire

1. How many alcoholic drinks did you have yesterday? This past week (including those already counted)? How many times did you drink in the last 3 months? In the past 6 months (including those already counted)?

2. Were medical issues addressed during your intake or during therapy? Was follow-up contact made for you by medical services? Was the program helpful in coordinating, planning, or educating you for medical care? Did you have a health care provider before you came to the alcohol service? Do you have one now? What is this person's specialty? Doctor or nurse?

3. How many times had you been in alcohol treatment before coming to HCHS? How many times since? Why did you seek care from an agency specializing in alcohol? Why did you come to a gay-identified agency? How did HCHS/HATS help you? How did HCHS/HATS fail you?

4. Was your treatment goal abstinence or controlled drinking? If abstinence, what has been your longest period of abstinence since treatment here? Before coming here? If controlled drinking, describe your drinking habits, frequency, quantity, and occasions.

5. If you had prior treatment for alcohol in nongay-identified agencies, would you describe your experiences as effective or noneffective? Or as helping you meet your goals or not? Can you give an example of why you answered as you did?

6. How were you referred to HCHS?

7. When were your treatment starting and ending dates?

8. What did you hope to accomplish in your treatment here?

ALCOHOLICS ANONYMOUS
AND THE GAY ALCOHOLIC

William E. Bittle, PhD

ABSTRACT. Although the number of homosexual alcoholic men and women has been estimated to be proportionately three times greater than the number of alcoholics in the general population, their participation in Alcoholics Anonymous is not consistent with this proportional representation. It is proposed that there are a number of characteristics of AA, as it is represented in meetings, which discourage participation by gay people. These characteristics are reviewed, and suggestions are made for providing homosexual alcoholics with support and with the tools for reasonably secure sobriety.

Given current estimates of the prevalance of alcohol abuse among homosexuals, statistics estimating the proportion of homosexuals within the general population, and personal and anecdotal experiences, it seems evident that, with the exception of large cities with identified gay Alcoholics Anonymous groups, AA has not attracted representative numbers of homosexual alcoholics. While this observation cannot be further substantiated, given the obstacles to data collection presented by AA's tradition of anonymity, it correlates with the findings of counselors and therapists that traditional strategems and resources for treatment are underutilized by gay men and women.

Many gay people who have made contact with AA express the feeling that they are not welcome. Lacking the encouragement to deal with their affectional preferences in a forthright manner, they typically withdraw from AA and return to drinking. This suggests that certain characteristics of Alcoholics Anonymous are experienced by gay people as hostile or unattractive, and that AA appears to them to offer little hope for the solution of their problems.[1]

This paper will take inventory of several characteristics of AA and will suggest how the principles of AA may be presented to gay men and women

---

Dr. Bittle is Professor, Department of Anthropology, University of Oklahoma, Norman, OK 73019.

[1]This represents the author's perspective in this paper. For other views of the involvement of homosexuals in AA see "The Homosexual Alcoholic" (available from The Hazelden Foundation, P.O. Box 176, Center City, MN 55012) or "A Gay Member's Eye View of Alcoholics Anonymous" (reprints from National Association of Gay Alcoholism Professionals, 204 West 20th St., New York, NY 10011) (Editors' note).

without distortion or modification, but in ways that may be perceived as attractive and potentially rewarding. The Eleventh Tradition of AA[2] suggests that the relationship of the Fellowship with others should be "one of attraction rather than promotion" (Bill W., 1955, p. 9). It would appear that an increase in the "attractiveness" of the program to gay men and women would only serve the best interests of both AA and gay alcoholics.

A major issue confronting every newcomer to the AA program is the frequent insistence by AA members that alcohol is the ultimate leveller: individual factors in personality, values, and background, and those other factors which are generally regarded as psychologically significant are for the most part irrelevant in "working the program." Whether or not such a claim is ultimately true (i.e., whether individual differences must be taken into account in the direct treatment of the primary symptom of alcoholism) is for the most part beside the point. For as Smith has pointed out in this volume, both the unique aspects of the gay subculture and the degree to which gay men and women vary from traditional thought and values instill homosexuals with the conviction that they are different in important ways. This conviction of "difference" is one that has generally been reinforced throughout their lives by almost everyone around them, and "being different" often becomes central in the philosophy of many gay men and women.

When AA members emphasize the "nonuniqueness" of the individual, they are doing so in the spirit of an egalitarian fellowship. Differences in income, education, drinking background, ethnic heritage, gender, and present condition are minimized in an effort to make the newcomer feel at home. The intent is to force the newcomer to focus on the shared problem of alcoholism, rather than on social differences which may inhibit full integration into the group. In addition, the stress on similarity is a critical component of ego reduction utilized by AA and all traditional alcoholism therapies are aimed at stripping the individual of the rigid, symptomatic denial that permits continued rationalization of drinking behavior.

For gay men and women, however, "different" almost automatically refers to their sexual and affectional preferences. Upon first contact with AA, then, most homosexuals will deny the claims that there are no differences between themselves and heterosexual individuals, that they have somehow erroneously interpreted the experiences of their lifetime, or that their distinctiveness, which has been generated, nurtured, and often grudgingly harbored, is invalid. A minimization of these differences seems equivalent to dismissing a critical component of their personality.

In a typical AA meeting, the approach to the solution of personal problems is through the exchange of ideas and experiences among members. Such ex-

---

[2]The Steps and Traditions are cornerstones of the AA program. See the references listed at the end of this article for a more complete understanding.

changes are liberally interspersed with references to the principles of AA and the Steps of the program. When a homosexual man or woman is involved in a small group discussion with heterosexual alcoholics, however, it often seems apparent that few members can deal competently or convincingly with affectional differences. No amount of abstract reassurance that "all of our problems are the same" will in fact address the problems perceived by the gay person as distinctly different, a disparity constantly reinforced by society at large.

The failure of many AA members to accept uniqueness, to say nothing of demeaning those who cling to what is often called "the illusion of being different," may hopelessly alienate the gay man or woman. As a functional compromise, many homosexuals maintain silence about their sexuality and about all other aspects of their lives that they perceive to be closely tied to that sexuality. They consequently deal overtly only with superficialities in their existence, substitute inaccurate or ambiguous pronouns when discussing love relationships, and in general maintain the same aloofness from other AA members that they have maintained from heterosexuals throughout their lives.

It is not uncommon for a gay man or woman who has participated in the program for several months, even years, and who has developed a degree of self-acceptance as a recovering alcoholic (though not necessarily as a gay human being) to indicate that under no circumstances would he or she reveal sexual preferences at a meeting—or even to a single member of their AA group—so strongly negative is the anticipated response. Gay men and women often privately indicate that one of their greatest fears is being "discovered" and no longer being accepted by other group members. Personal honesty, much stressed in AA, becomes something of a travesty for the gay individual who is "passing" as heterosexual. The simple guilt of not being open with persons with whom close ties are developing is added to the accumulated guilt of years of drinking.

In spite of the attitudes expressed by members of AA, little in the AA literature actually suggests that individuals in the program must abdicate their sense of uniqueness in order to achieve sobriety. "Unity" (one of the legacies of the Fellowship) does not imply uniformity. The Sixth and Seventh Steps of the program, which concern elimination of "character defects," suggest that important changes must be made by each individual in his view of himself and others. But there is hardly the mandate that characteristics as basic as sexual orientation must be changed or expunged. Quite the contrary, the literature stresses the importance of tailoring a program which is appropriate to the life-style of the individual. The Steps are called "suggestions" for recovery, and the *Grapevine,* a monthly AA publication, devotes almost all of its space to articles by people who share the many ways in which they have interpreted the Steps in applying them to their own lives. Nonetheless, many members of AA who have themselves achieved sobriety through highly personalized internalization of the principles of the Fellowship, tend to assume that their own methods represent a fail-safe, immutable formula for newcomers. When this personal format is inflexible and does not accept individual differences, the program becomes much less attractive to those gay men and women who know that differences exist between themselves and others.

Another problem which gay people have encountered in AA and about which they are frequently highly critical outside of meetings is the apparent hard core puritanism of many AA members. Despite the fact that Bill W. suggests in his prolific writings that fear, anger, and sex are the three most troublesome areas of the alcoholic's personality—underlying many other "character defects" and contributing to the self-destructive behavior of drinking— sex is rarely discussed at AA meetings. More than this, sex is almost never discussed during "social periods" before and after meetings. If the topic of sex is raised, members of AA and sponsors of newly entering men and women often suggest that sexual abstinence be maintained for periods ranging from several months to a year. The clear implication is that recovery is difficult if not impossible if one attempts to deal at the same time with one's sexuality. An equally compelling argument might be made that sobriety is difficult for the gay man or woman to achieve *without* at the same time dealing with his or her sexual preferences. For a great many gay alcoholics, sexuality has been seen as a "reason" for drinking, and if some inroads into this aspect of the problem cannot be made at an early stage, an unnecessary burden is placed on the individual.

Although lifelong sexual abstinence is not suggested as a prerequisite for continued sobriety, it is often claimed that sex will remain a major problem in the lives of recovering alcoholics and may constitute a continuing threat to sobriety. An article in the *Grapevine* expresses the viewpoint of many members of AA. The author quotes an old timer as having said, "There's only one thing that'll ever get you drunk in this program—Sex." (Anon., 1978, p. 8).

AA members may also suggest that if one "works the program" effectively, sexual problems will vanish. This is certainly a dubious psychological proposition, and the mere suggestion is often enough to turn a gay person from the program. In a number of instances, where gay recovering alcoholics have attempted to reconcile their sexual preference and have solicited assistance from sponsors or other members of the group, they have been told that their affectional orientation is just "one more defect of character" that will be removed if the Sixth and Seventh Steps are properly taken. The attitudes of individual AA members again do not accurately reflect the philosophy of Alcoholics Anonymous but only the diverse ways in which individuals interpret that philosophy. Alternative modes for dealing with sexual problems and remaining sober are numerous, and the homosexual alcoholic should have access to those modes that fit his or her own particular needs.

In summary, the general impression that one may obtain by attending AA meetings is that sex is to be heavily restricted or ignored until other "more important" problems have been resolved. One may even gain the impression that one's sexual problems are part of a core of problems that will remain for some undefined but significant period of time unapproachable and immutable. Relatively few gay men and women find the implied monasticism of this attitude especially appealing. Additionally, one may get the idea that if sex as a heterosexual phenomenon is something to be avoided in conversation, then homosexual sex must certainly constitute unspeakable behavior. The gay member, then, is reinforced in a belief that his or her homosexuality would threaten a relationship with the group if disclosed. It may be argued that such puritanism is unrealistic for any recovering alcoholic, since there is ample evidence that sexual problems are among the most significant ones in the lives of most alcoholics. Weinberg (1977) discusses the problems of guilt, low sexual self-esteem, impotence, performance fears, and other characteristics of the alcoholic in recovery. In a preface, he too acknowledges the fact that "sex has been too much of a taboo topic in alcohol and drug treatment programs," and that "little attention has been paid to the sexual needs of those people in recovery from chemical dependency" (p. 4).

A third area with which gay women and men find difficulty in their early and often continuing encounters with AA (and again, this is not limited to gay people) is the spiritual part of the program. Bell and Weinberg (1978) summarize their findings on the attitudes of gay men and women as confirming "to a limited extent others' findings and impressions that homosexual adults tend to be more alienated from formal religion than are heterosexuals" (p. 153). Many gay men and women have found that one of the major factors in the development of their guilt about their sexual preference has come from organized religion, and many gay alcoholics, therefore, arrive in the AA program with more hostility than indifference to religion. Five of AA's Twelve Steps make direct reference to "God" or "Him," and another step refers to a "Power" that is widely interpreted by members of the Fellowship as equivalent to an orthodox "God." The writings of AA's co-founder, Bill W., are liberally sprinkled with references to "God," and his own orientation clearly was strongly religious. Even a cursory reading of the "Big Book" (*Alcoholics Anonymous*, Anonymous, 1939), *Twelve Steps and Twelve Traditions* (Anonymous, 1952), *The AA Way of Life* (Bill W., 1967), and other AA publications leaves little doubt that in spite of the emphasized qualification of the Third and Eleventh Steps, "God, as we understood Him" (1952, p. 59), the founders of AA and a major fraction of the membership regard this "power" as a more or less orthodox religious concept.

When a religious nonbeliever comes into the program and is candid, established members frequently express feelings ranging from outright alarm to condescension. New members are routinely assured that a belief in "God" is not important in the first few weeks or months of recovery, since it is the members' general experience that newcomers have difficulty with religion, yet it is just as routinely argued that, with time, a concept of "God" will develop. Strong pressures are put upon the newcomer to make the establishment of this belief a priority. Experience with successfully recovering members of AA who are disbelievers at entry and remain so through lengthy periods of sobriety would indicate that an espousal of a supernatural power, or of any surrogate in this realm, is not in fact necessary for recovery. Nonbelievers can utilize the program effectively and can develop "spiritually" if that term is interpreted only as individual growth and change. In two relatively inconspicuous places in the AA literature, Bill W. recognizes this fact, although these citations are rarely provided to the newcomer. (See Anonymous, 1955, p. 570; Anonymous, 1957, p. 167.)

A final problem manifested in AA meetings is excessive and often cult-like orthodoxy. Absolute and unvarying conformity to what is said to be in the AA literature is argued as the sine qua non of recovery from alcoholism. Since these materials are generally first encountered by a newcomer as presented orally in meetings, he or she is exposed more to personal interpretations than to the actual sources. Despite routine disclaimers, speakers at AA meetings present the program less as "suggested" means of recovery than as a set of invariable rules. The basic notion communicated is "If you don't work the program as I have worked the program, then you won't get sober." It is typical, for example, for participants at an AA meeting to remark that they "have never met anyone who continued to maintain contacts with old friends (or who went to bars, or who took medication, or who smoked pot, or who used poppers) who stayed sober." Since most of these comments are without foundation in fact and since many are also distortions of the recommendations in the AA literature, the newcomer recognizes them as such and tends to dismiss not only the extravagant statements but the substance of the program as well.

For the gay man or woman coming into AA, the statements by older members regarding the lengths to which they go to avoid situations in which alcohol is present seem absurd. On the one hand, the newcomer is told that the desire to drink will leave him but on the other, many members of AA devote considerable time to the discussion of the extremes to which they have gone to avoid contact with "old drinking buddies" and "slippery" situations where liquor is present. That such measures may well be necessary in the early period of abstinence is reasonable. Yet to the gay newcomer, confronted with a number of people who appear to have become literally "professional" recovering alcoholics, AA seems less a program aimed at recovery and reintegration into society than a step toward taking the veil.[3]

---

[3]A sharp divergence of gay AA members from program orthodoxy is the matter of socializing in gay bars. See the preceding paper by Ronnie Colcher for further discussion (Editors' note).

Typically, the AA literature is noncommittal with respect to many of the specifics that are dealt with authoritatively in meetings and tends to summarize experience rather than to mandate practices. This seems an important point to stress to the gay newcomer, along with strong encouragement to utilize those materials which are pertinent to his or her own life. Unlike a theological system, which may be said to address the masses, AA addresses the individual, and it is perhaps this very characteristic of flexibility that has permitted it to serve such a diverse group of people as it has during more than 45 years of existence.

Conclusion

It might seem from the foregoing discussion that Alcoholics Anonymous is not of service to the gay alcoholic, but this conclusion would be false. The basic tenets of the Fellowship, the guidelines and suggestions that it offers in the area of treatment of the primary symptom of alcoholism, and the support which it affords in treating this malady are probably without parallel. Several suggestions are appropriate, however, and these are designed to help both the gay alcoholic and those working with gay alcoholics to derive the greatest benefits from AA.

The early acquisition of an AA sponsor who is either gay or who is altogether comfortable with and knowledgeable about gay men and women is of prime importance. The obvious function of a sponsor is to "funnel" the materials of AA to the individual and to do so in meaningful ways which permit the individual to handle effectively the problems of recovery. Without this type of assistance, the gay person encounters a seemingly alien and irrelevant environment and often opts to leave, finding little hope in such surroundings.

Second, it must be assumed that a majority of gay women and men coming into AA will need more than the AA group if their continued sobriety is to be successful and reasonably secure. Many of the problems which they bring with them will not be considered in AA meetings, and it is imperative that they maintain contact with gay support groups. Gay AA groups, where they can be found, are enormously helpful in a broader sense, but in most areas of the country additional support must be sought from other sources, such as gay consciousness raising groups or gay counselors. Outreach programs specifically designed to assist members of the gay community are also clearly important. It is improbable that Alcoholics Anonymous will itself provide such programs in the near future, since AA's policy is "attraction rather than promotion." Such outreach programs need not violate the spirit of AA's Traditions.

Finally, a program of education both within and outside of AA seems urgent. The degree of ignorance of the problems of gay men and women and the homophobia which is too often expressed by members of AA are but reflections of popular notions about gay people. Education may be accomplished within AA by gay women and men who are secure in their sobriety and comfortable with their sexuality.

Although it may be true that Alcoholics Anonymous has perhaps the best "track record" of any organization involving recovery from alcoholism, there is little point in maintaining the pretense that its success with gay men and women is correspondingly good. Homosexual alcoholics have certain needs that are distinct from heterosexual alcoholics, and homosexual alcoholics may well need support beyond that to be found in the Fellowship. To ignore these facts is to ignore the needs of significant numbers of highly productive men and women.

REFERENCES

Anonymous. *Alcoholics Anonymous* (1st ed.). New York: Works Publishing, Inc., 1939.

Anonymous. *Twelve steps and twelve traditions*. New York: Alcoholics Anonymous World Services, 1952.

Anonymous. *Alcoholics Anonymous* (2nd ed.). New York: Alcoholics Anonymous World Services, 1955.

Anonymous. *Alcoholics Anonymous comes of age*. New York: Alcoholics Anonymous World Services, 1957.

Anonymous. Sex is not the answer. *Grapevine*, August 1978, 8-11.

Bell, A. P., & Weinberg, M. S. *Homosexualities: A study of diversity among men and women.* New York: Simon and Schuster, 1978.

W., Bill. *A.A. tradition: How it developed*. New York: Alcoholics Anonymous World Services, 1955.

W., Bill. *The A.A. way of life*. New York: Alcoholics Anonymous World Services, 1967.

Weinberg, J. R. *Sex and recovery*. Minneapolis: Recovery Press, 1977.

PREVENTING ALCOHOL ABUSE
IN THE GAY COMMUNITY:
TOWARD A THEORY AND MODEL

John E. Mongeon
Thomas O. Ziebold, PhD

ABSTRACT. Urban gay communities present unique populations for a comprehensive prevention program. They are well defined, bounded communities with rapid internal communication, can be considered "at risk" for alcoholism, and are traditionally "underserved" for prevention and treatment. Models of alcoholism epidemiology elucidate critical factors relevant to the urban gay population, and indigenous gay organizations afford effective means of implementing a program. The model presented in this paper is based upon current research about successful prevention programs and uses accepted strategies tailored to the specific characteristics of the urban gay community. The basic premise of the model is that community self help is the most effective approach to alcohol and drug abuse prevention.

The cornerstone for a model of preventing alcohol abuse within the gay community is the concept of self-help: gay people taking the responsbility for altering their own behavioral norms in relation to alcohol, both individually and as a community. We believe that a prevention/early intervention program created *within* the community, to meet its own perceived needs, stands a much greater chance of being accepted and effective. Our model would utilize existing community resources and institutions wherever possible—human service, communications networks, service, social and special interest groups—throughout the program's development and implementation. Involving the "rank and file" as well as the leadership of the gay community and mobilizing volunteer resources could ensure this program's success.

Our efforts to prevent alcoholism and alcohol abuse capitalize upon a history of gay people taking care of their own health needs by organizing to control the spread of venereal disease. The Public Health Service has recognized the role of the volunteer gay community in reducing a health problem of major proportions through VD testing and control programs developed and staffed by gay volunteers. We believe that the same vigorous self-help approach can be used to intervene in and greatly reduce the present high risk of alcoholism among

---

The authors' affiliations and addresses are listed in the footnote of the introductory paper.

gays. The preliminary experiences of the Whitman-Walker Clinic's Gay Counsel on Drinking Behavior and the phenomenal growth of gay chapters of Alcoholics Anonymous in the metropolitan Washington, D.C. area over the past few years substantiate that belief.

The use of a self-help model has the adventage of achieving a unique fit of program to population. The growing awareness of the hazards of alcohol abuse within the gay community is evidenced by major feature articles in San Francisco's *Advocate* (Shilts, 1976); Washington, D.C.'s *The Blade* (Ziebold, 1978); Boston's *Gay Community News* (McGirr & Skinner, 1974); and the New York-based *Christopher Street* magazine.

It can be argued that this type of community-based program is the only approach likely to make significant inroads into the problem of destructive alcohol use among gay people. Many gays are suspicious and distrustful of traditional health and human service agencies. Therefore, more traditional prevention and early intervention approaches—utilizing those institutions and communications networks from which the young urban gay man or woman has generally been isolated—will have little impact. On the other hand, just as the gay community is recognized as a leader in the control and reduction of venereal diseases, it is likely that

> the gay subculture might be a creative leader in solving another public-health problem that our larger society has successfully managed to ignore. It would not be the first time that a viable minority, acting out of a need to preserve its own identity and fulfill its own destiny, has shown the majority how to take effective social action. (Ziebold, 1979, p. 44)

Approach to Alcoholism Prevention for Gays

The authors of this paper characterize the sexual minority population as one definitely "at risk" with beverage alcohol. The specific characteristics of that population, in light of current sociological models for alcoholism and emotional distress, point the way to developing effective prevention and early intervention programs. C. R. Snyder (1959) developed a sociological view of alcoholism that establishes three major variables affecting a group's drinking behavior: "dynamic factors" that define the level of acute psychic tension in the group; "normative factors" that define norms, sentiments and ideas about drinking embedded in cultural traditions of the group; and "alternative factors," all culturally patterned behaviors other than excessive drinking that may be equivalent as modes of adjustment to acute emotional stress. In Snyder's words,

> This scheme suggests that alcoholism involves a convergence of acute psychic tension. . .with a particular attitude toward drinking presumably communicated to the individual by the other members of the group. And

it supposes that the individual's situation becomes structured so as to close off the alternative modes of adjustment. (p. 34)

This logical model conforms in all respects to problems that are particularly evident within the homosexual subculture. As Ziebold (1979) noted, "The risk for gay persons in an oppressive society is that they become vulnerable to addictive behavior as a mechanism for relieving anxiety and pain" (p. 39).

Snyder's model suggests a strategy of prevention aimed at reducing the psychic stress of the urban gay man or woman by providing coping alternatives and also by influencing the "normative factors" within the gay community which either condone or promote excessive consumption of beverage alcohol. In terms of the traditional public health model of disease control, we propose both to increase the resistance of the "host" and reduce the adverse characteristics of the urban gay environment (or the "gay ghetto," as it is sometimes called) which perpetuate a climate of alcohol misuse and dependence.

Current thinking about primary prevention recognizes the validity and indeed the desirability of a dual focus on both the individual and his or her social context. The August 17, 1979 Prevention Policy Paper of the Alcohol, Drug Abuse and Mental Health Administration (ADAMHA) concluded:

Policymakers should consider intervention approaches embracing a broader context with the aim of improving social and environmental conditions. Such an approach complements intervention at the individual/family level and offers the greatest potential for enhancing human functioning.

The President's Commission on Mental Health (PCMH) also recognized the necessity of addressing prevention activities to the social and cultural context of the individual, as well as to his or her personal psychological or developmental issues. They recognized:

the harmful effect that a variety of social, environmental, physical, psychological, and biological factors can have on the ability of individuals to function in society, develop a sense of their own worth and maintain a strong and purposeful self-image. (Bryant et al., 1978, p. 9)

George Albee (Note 1), Professor of Psychology at the University of Vermont and Coordinator of the Task Panel on Prevention for the PCMH, has attempted to synthesize these complex variables into a prevention hypothesis which embodies the prevention strategy we are proposing.

The conditions associated with higher rates of emotional distress and substance abuse constitute a set of interrelated factors that include stress, competence, self-esteem, support groups, and feelings of personal power. . . .

The following formula helps pull together a number of different research findings related to the incidence of emotional distress, and thus has important implications for prevention:

$$\text{Incidence} = \frac{\text{Organic factors} + \text{stress}}{\text{Competence} + \text{Self-esteem} + \text{Support groups}}$$

If one's purpose is to reduce incidence through primary prevention efforts, one may adopt the strategy of: (1) reducing factors in the numerator, or (2) increasing factors in the denominator. (p. 14)

The intervention approach we believe best fits with this conceptualization aims at decreasing incidence of alcohol misuse within the urban gay male and female communities by: (1) improving the coping skills and competencies of individuals, (2) attempting to influence the norms of the community by providing alternate outlets for recreation and socialization, and (3) heightening the community consciousness and sense of responsibility around the destructive use of alcohol by its members.

The predominant characteristics of this model in many ways closely match the prevention philosophies and strategies advocated by representatives of ethnic and racial minorities, such as the Center for Multicultural Awareness funded by the National Institute on Drug Abuse. The Center recognizes the need to build prevention programs within the contexts of particular communities or cultures; to utilize the values, resources and institutions of that culture; and also to address the complex issues of personal choice and decision-making involved in simultaneously living within, among, and between a variety of cultures. As Gary Weaver of the PRIDE/American University noted (1975), "No longer are individuals denying their identities to fit into an abstractive, Anglo-male [heterosexual] society. They are asserting their uniqueness and wholeness while taking it for granted that they are entitled to their fair share of society's benefits" (p. 377). Carolyn Payton (Note 2), former director of the Center for Multicultural Awareness, commented: "For policy makers to continue to believe and behave as though prejudice and oppression are insignificantly related to the drug problems of minorities is a farce" (p. 7).

Gary Weaver's rather optimistic analysis gives token recognition to the similarity of the "Gay Lib" movement in confronting issues of affiliation and involvement with heterosexual communities and simultaneous involvement in the homosexual community. Yet it begs the question of continuous conflict over self-affirmation which the gay man or woman confronts.

Edmund White, a prominent gay author and novelist, has written, "To become gay, to acknowledge being gay, is a way of inventing yourself and, in a sense, being reborn. . . .Once you find you are gay, every part of your existence has to be reinvented" (1980, p. 16). That option of "passing" as heterosexual to any or all of the world, the consistent choice of self-affirmation or self-denial, is a confusing and often painful one for many gay men and women. The confusion and pain is also intensified by the feelings of isolation and aloneness in that struggle; gays are the only minority group whose parents do not even share that sense of "being different." So again, that cultural experience of "asserting uniqueness and wholeness" is absent; in its place is that sense of inadequacy, loneliness, and guilt that leads many human beings, regardless of sexual preference, into alcoholism.

Dr. Stephen Glenn (Note 3) points out seven developmental characteristics that can be found in "well-adjusted" individuals. In general, the "high risk" individual (for chemical dependency) showed significant inadequacies in one, several or all the following areas: (1) identification with viable role models, (2) identification with and responsibility for "family" processes (family is used here in the broadest sense), (3) low faith in "miracle" solutions to problems, (4) adequate intra-personal skills, (5) adequate inter-personal skills, (6) skills dealing with systems, and (7) judgemental skills.

Gay people's difficulties in developing needed competence and coping skills, while confronting a sense of isolation and separation from those individuals and institutions usually responsible for instilling those skills, should be evident. Therefore, our intervention approach would assist individuals "at risk" with alcohol by increasing their sense of self and by enabling them to make more responsible determinations of their own roles, values, and behaviors, including the consumption of alcohol.

The creation of alternative support systems as a strategy for promoting both self-worth and health-enhancing behaviors is also a well-documented approach to alcohol abuse prevention. The theme of providing women with additional options for their lives runs through the growing literature on women and alcohol. Sharon Wilsnack, one of the pioneers in the field of women's alcoholism, writes

> We must open options to women earlier in their lives, and make them realize that they can choose what they will be, that anything is possible. . . when neither women nor men feel the pressure to fit into artificial roles, I think some of the tension will be reduced that contributes to alcoholism. (1976, p. 42)

This observation seems particularly appropriate to urban gay men and women, who are also steeped in sex-stereotyped roles and behaviors, both inside and outside the gay community. Developing support systems seems particularly applicable to a target population both isolated from traditional support and devoid of constructive role models during conventional interactions in subcultural meeting places, e.g., bars, baths, bookstores, and public places.

Our intervention approach, then, draws upon the body of knowledge developing around effective substance abuse prevention strategies designed to promote personal coping and competence skills, provides constructive outlets for socialization and recreation, builds strong support networks for positive reinforcement of constructive behavior, and includes the recognition that prevention strategies must be constructed upon and within the values, norms, institutions, and rituals of the target community. Finally, this approach also recognizes that the cornerstone of prevention programs that are likely to be sustained is a strategy that invites community responsibility for its own physical and mental health.

The Early Intervention Program

We propose an early intervention program designed to enhance the coping and competence skills of gay men and women by providing them the opportunity to participate in a 36 hour, 12 week structured program. Recognizing that a variety of intra- and interpersonal skills contribute to an individual's ability to function comfortably within the gay subculture and in relation to the larger society, we propose to test a variety of self-enhancement strategies in our group experience. These include interpersonal communications/assertiveness, values clarification, decision making (applied to both alcohol-related situations and other personal/social choices), life review, skills inventory, career planning, journaling and role-playing, each tailored to the needs and concerns of each group.

In terms of the organization and conduct of the group sessions, we believe the following practices will contribute to their success:

1. Voluntary participation. Although individuals identified as particularly at risk may be encouraged to participate, recruiting emphasis will be on meeting the needs of those who want to join the program.
2. The groups would be conducted by trained volunteers from within the gay community. We see this as critical to building trust and credibility within the groups.
3. The tone and climate of each group would be positive and supportive, encouraging each participant to recognize and effectively utilize his own problem solving skills.
4. The sessions would allow each participant to explore his or her own uniqueness, and encourage individual decisions around life-style and behavioral issues.

The general goals of the intervention program would be to increase the self-esteem and coping skills of gay men and women. As Nathaniel Branden described in *The Disowned Self* (1971, p. 23), we seek to increase personal and social awareness, acceptance, assertiveness and responsibility in order to prevent the development of a dependence on beverage alcohol.

The proposed program would involve a three hour session once each week for twelve weeks. The participatory and experiential sessions involve handouts, exercises, role plays, and written assignments to facilitate the process of self-examination and redirection. Training curriculum might incorporate an individually tailored mix of:

— *Life Review*: using fantasy, life-line plotting, significant incident inventories, stepping stones, and metaphor to focus participants on the experiences of their own lives.
— *Strengths and Resource Inventories*: building upon the life review data to increase the participants' awareness of their own positive accomplishments, attributes, and aptitudes.
— *Telling the Tale*: journal-keeping and sharing of personal experiences to enable participants to begin building closer relationships with other gay people.
— *Assertiveness*: building upon the assumption that everyone has the right to possess and express his or her own feelings to give participants additional coping skills in the wider society, as well as within the gay subculture itself.
— *Sexual Styles Awareness and Creative Intimacy*: applying the values clarification activities and principles of assertiveness to the sexual arena, a particularly troublesome one for single gay men and women.
— *Goal-Setting*: using directed exercises to begin focussing participants on personal and professional goals which are broken down into specific achievable objectives and the necessary steps toward those goals.
— *Support System Building*: encouraging participants to begin intentionally broadening and strengthening their interpersonal support network, both for the achievement of specific goals and for emotional nurturance and growth.
— *Life Planning*: using the information and goal-setting skills generated earlier to enable participants to work constructively toward the future.
— *Decisions in Drinking*: incorporating material from the National Center for Alcohol Education series throughout the group experience so participants can begin to assess the role of alcohol in their personal and social choices and behavior.

The Outreach Program

A second, critical component of our prevention model is the creation of a more supportive environment for program participants and others as they begin to alter their patterns of alcohol use. Two factors in the gay experience may impede and frustrate this change: the relative isolation and loneliness of "at risk" individuals and the focus of the gay life-style on settings and activities where alcohol is featured.

Although the kind of intensive group program we have described is expected to help at-risk gay persons begin to alter their life-styles with respect to alcohol, these efforts are not likely to be successful unless changes also occur in the everyday environment of the gay community. Furthermore, no intervention program can expect to serve all of those who may need assistance. Many individuals may not want or be able to spend the time and energy needed; others may not recognize the extent of their own misuse of alcohol or the threat of alcoholism to their well-being. For both of these reasons, we believe a community-directed outreach program will help support and extend what can be accomplished in the group sessions.

We also are convinced that the logic of self-help will make it possible for intervention program participants to help change the drinking norms of the gay community by providing the leverage needed to influence a far greater number of gays than could participate directly. The gay community already is developing a variety of social, religious, political, and service organizations that could serve both as alternatives to the gay bar environment and as sources of support to those who choose to reduce their use of alcohol. Through the initiative of program participants, we can begin to generate a pool of gay men and women with a heightened consciousness of the destructive consequences of gay alcohol abuse who can carry their new norms into the larger gay community.

At the same time, we propose a direct impact on the alcohol-promoting norms of the gay community by conducting a community education/outreach campaign to be planned, developed, and implemented by the gay community itself. By including representatives of gay organizations, gay media (*The Blade, Out,* and the "Friends" radio show), and also gay bar owners, we would create a target-specific effort that is both satisfying and effective. We envision utilizing traditional outreach approaches, i.e., posters, ads, and speakers bureaus, but also developing innovative educational strategies. Two examples may help highlight our approach:

First, the owner of a large "glitter" bar in the Washington area is considering providing alternative settings within a successful bar: separate space where alcohol is not served, hours during which alcoholic drinks will not be served, reduction in the price of nonalcoholic drinks, bartender education about alcoholism and alcoholic drinking patterns, altering the bar mood at certain times to "bring down" the clientele, and other strategies. This owner is willing to participate in demonstrations to assess the effectiveness of alcohol abuse reduction consistent with operating a sound, profitable business. We learned from this discussion that the avenue to explore is the effect of current wars among gay bars to attract customers, efforts which are, of course, "subsidizing" the heavy drinker. This owner would be willing to evaluate volume-price relationships and alternate proposals (through promotion, community activities using his bar, and so on) as an adjunct to an alcohol abuse prevention model.

Such an approach would be based on the recognition of two realities: (1) The gay bar is a central feature of the gay community, and it may be easier to alter people's drinking habits within the setting of the gay bar than to attract them to another activity altogether. (2) While bars are businesses that must make a profit to remain open, we are convinced that cappucino, Perrier water, fruit drinks, and other nonalcoholic beverages can produce a profit if the demand for them is encouraged.

Second, we suggest the conduct of alcohol awareness training sessions for various "gatekeepers" within the community, including not only bartenders, but also hair stylists, gym attendants, bath employees, and bookstore clerks. This training would enlist the cooperation of these individuals in their regular contact with large segments of the gay community (who may not be reached through other outreach efforts) to:

1. recognize individuals whose behavior, conversation or demeanor indicate some present difficulty with beverage alcohol;
2. intervene constructively, perhaps by suggesting some nonthreatening avenues for help or putting the individual in contact with this project;
3. support the efforts of this project to reduce the excessive consumption of alcohol in the gay community by using their influence as role models to set examples.

Experience from the earlier successful efforts of the gay community to halt the rising rate of venereal disease also is applicable here. Posters such as "GAY LOVE NEEDS CARE," now more than 10 years old, are still evident within the gay community. Gay bars and baths were willing to cooperate in screening and testing efforts (the Whitman-Walker Clinic still conducts regular VD screenings for interested individuals at local gay baths on regularly scheduled evenings).

As a consequence of these efforts, we believe it would be possible to:

1. develop a significant pool of "positive role models" within the community, individuals whose lives are not inextricably linked with obsessive consumption of alcohol;
2. create additional, as well as strengthen existing, alternative social, political, cultural, and religious outlets within the gay community for individuals to meet their personal and social needs;
3. increase awareness within the gay community of the negative consequences of obsessive alcohol consumption, and a cultural stance which discourages rather than fosters such behavior;
4. reduce the number of individuals within the community involved in self-

destructive behavior associated with obsessive consumption of beverage alcohol.

Then, as a result of these changes, we believe the model program would have impact in the form of:

1. significant and measurable changes in the consumption of beverage alcohol in the gay community;
2. increasing visibility of alternatives to social activities that do not center on alcohol consumption;
3. shifts in norms within the gay community away from the present emphasis on, and use of, alcohol in social settings.

Our long-term objectives are ambitious. However, in developing this model, we view the gay community as a subculture in the process of developing and defining its own cultural values and norms. We see this conceptualization as an attempt to contribute to the inculcation of a series of positive attitudes around the role of alcohol in the lives of community members. Our approach aims at fostering the development of new cultural values regarding responsible and moderate consumption of beverage alcohol in an environment where a variety of nonalcohol-dependent outlets for socialization and growth can be readily available to community members.

REFERENCE NOTES

1. Albee, G. Preventing primary prevention. In H. S. Resnik (Ed.), *Primary prevention and health promotion*. Unpublished monograph developed for the National Institute on Drug Abuse, 5600 Fishers Lane, Rockville, MD 20857.
2. Payton, C. Multicultural issues in drug abuse prevention. Paper presented at the First Annual Alcohol, Drug Abuse and Mental Health Administration Prevention Conference, Silver Spring, MD, September 21, 1979.
3. Glenn, S. *The developmental approach in preventing problem dependencies.* Book in preparation, 1980.

REFERENCES

Alcohol, Drug Abuse and Mental Health Administration. *Prevention policy paper.* Rockville, MD: ADAMHA, September 21, 1979.
Branden, N. *The disowned self.* New York: Nash Publishing Co., 1971.
Bryant, T. R., et al. *Report of the President's commission on mental health* (Vol. 1). Washington, D.C.: U.S. Government Printing Office, 1978.
McGirr, K., & Skinner, R. Alcohol use and abuse in the gay community: A view toward alternatives. *Gay Community News,* May/June 1974.
Shilts, R. Alcoholism: A look in depth at how a national menace is affecting the gay community. *The Advocate,* February 25, 1976, 16-25.
Snyder, C. R. A sociological view of the etiology of alcoholism. In D. J. Pittman (ED.), *Alcoholism: An interdisciplinary approach.* Springfield, IL: Charles C. Thomas, 1959.
Weaver, G. American identity movements: A cross-cultural confrontation. *Intellect,* March 1975.

White, E. *States of desire: Travels in gay America.* New York: E. P. Dutton, 1980.

Wilsnack, S. The impact of sex roles on women's alcohol use and abuse. In M. Greenblatt & M. A. Shuckit (Eds.), *Alcoholism problems in women and children.* New York: Grune & Stratton, 1976.

Ziebold, T. O. Alcoholism and the gay community. *The Blade,* March/April 1978.

Ziebold, T. O. Alcoholism and recovery: Gays helping gays. *Christopher Street,* January 1979, 36-44.

WORKING TOGETHER: THE NATIONAL ASSOCIATION OF GAY ALCOHOLISM PROFESSIONALS

Emily B. McNally, MEd, CAC
Dana G. Finnegan, PhD, CAC

ABSTRACT. This article briefly describes the formation of the National Association of Gay Alcoholism Professionals (NAGAP). It then discusses the need for education, information, and advocacy that prompted the development of NAGAP's goals. There are four primary goals: (1) creating and fostering a network for support and communication among gay and lesbian alcoholism professionals; (2) educating those who work with gay/lesbian alcoholics; (3) raising the gay and lesbian communities' consciousness about alcoholism; and (4) improving treatment for gay/lesbian alcoholics, partly through advocacy. NAGAP's ultimate goal is to serve as a national "voice of conscience for the whole alcoholism field."

On July 4, 1979, NAGAP—the National Association of Gay Alcoholism Professionals—was created by a group of 15 lesbian and gay male alcoholism professionals who were attending the Rutgers Summer School of Alcohol Studies in New Jersey. In the process of meeting and sharing with one another, these individuals discovered how isolated many of them felt in their professional careers and decided to establish a communication and support network.

Although the establishment of this network was the original creative impetus for NAGAP, it soon became apparent that NAGAP should and could address other pressing issues. These included the need for a national voice for gay alcoholism professionals, a national organization that could teach nongay alcoholism professionals about gay and lesbian lifestyles and special needs, a national group that could raise the gay community's consciousness about the problems of alcoholism, and a national voice that could speak for the needs and special problems of the gay alcoholic. Above and beyond these particular needs, however, was the primary one of confronting and breaking through society's and the alcoholism field's denial, negative attitudes, and misconceptions about gay men and lesbians.

Emily McNally and Dana Finnegan are the National Coordinators of the National Association of Gay Alcoholism Professionals and may be reached at 204 W. 20th St., New York, NY 10011.

With these needs in mind, the original members formulated the goals of NAGAP. The first goal is a network for support and communication among gay alcoholism professionals. This network consists of meetings for members whenever feasible (for example, at national conferences), a quarterly newsletter that reports on news and progress in the area of alcoholism and homosexuality, a national headquarters that puts members in touch with one another and provides information and organizational support, regional chapters, and an informal communication system of phone calls and letters.

Another goal is to educate members of organizations and agencies about gay people and alcoholism, to help them change their attitudes about gay people, and to assist them in dealing constructively with gay clients. This educational effort takes various forms. For example, NAGAP members present papers, workshops, and training seminars on gay alcoholism at agencies, conferences, and professional meetings. During 1981, NAGAP members delivered a paper at the annual Alcohol Forum of the National Council on Alcoholism in New Orleans, gave a two-day training on Counseling the Gay/Lesbian Alcoholic for the State of New Jersey, and presented workshops at the Third Annual Women in Crisis conference in New York City.

In addition, NAGAP acts as a clearinghouse for resource and research information in the field of alcoholism as it pertains to homosexuality. The organization provides referral information about gay groups of AA and Al-Anon and compiles and distributes a *Directory of Facilities and Services for Gay/Lesbian Alcoholics* (1981). NAGAP has also compiled and distributes the *NAGAP Bibliography: Resources on Alcoholism and Lesbians/Gay Men (1981),* the first comprehensive bibliography on the topic that makes available information which has been basically unavailable previously.

As part of its educational effort, NAGAP also encourages alcohol and drug studies schools and institutes to provide courses on "Counseling the Gay/Lesbian Alcoholic." As a result of NAGAP's efforts, a three-week course was offered at the 1981 Rutgers' Summer School of Alcohol Studies and will be offered again in 1982. The summer school of the University of California at Irvine has also introduced a seminar on this topic.

Raising the consciousness and combatting the stereotypes of nongay agencies and individuals is accomplished by publicizing the existence of NAGAP and by making gay alcoholism professionals more visible. While fully and carefully respecting the privacy of all persons who wish to remain anonymous, NAGAP encourages gay professionals to be open and visible. Many nongay professionals have commented especially on how important it has been for their own growth and understanding to meet and interact with healthy, integrated lesbian and gay male professionals.

A third goal of NAGAP's programs is to raise the gay community's consciousness and to combat its denial about the problem of alcoholism among gay people. NAGAP supports gay caucuses, task forces, and professional organizations in the health care field and educates other gay/lesbian health care professionals about alcoholism. Shortly after its formation, NAGAP joined and became active in the National Gay Health Coalition. NAGAP has supported the National Gay Task Force on Substance Abuse, the Lesbian Caucus of the Women in Crisis Conference, and the Gay Caucus of the National Association of Alcoholism Counselors. NAGAP has provided information for articles in gay newspapers, and individual NAGAP members present information on alcoholism to gay/lesbian political, social, and professional groups.

The fourth goal is that of improving treatment for gay alcoholic clients, a result that comes primarily from achieving the first three goals. In addition, NAGAP acts as a national voice of advocacy for gay/lesbian clients' rights. NAGAP has met with staff members of the National Institute on Alcohol Abuse and Alcoholism (NIAAA) to educate them about the severity of the alcoholism problem in the gay community and the needs of this community. NAGAP maintains working relationships with other national organizations such as the National Association of Alcoholism Counselors and the National Council on Alcoholism in order to facilitate its advocacy efforts.

Finally, NAGAP serves as a voice of conscience for the whole alcoholism field. By publicizing the specific alcoholism problems of the gay/lesbian community, by educating other professionals, and by encouraging high visibility of lesbian and gay male professionals, NAGAP encourages the whole alcoholism treatment community to recognize that lesbians and gay men exist, that they include alcoholics and co-alcoholics, and that they have special needs and problems.

REFERENCES

National Association of Gay Alcoholism Professionals. *Directory of facilities and services for gay/lesbian alcoholics.* NAGAP, 1981. (Available from NAGAP, 204 W. 20th St., New York, NY 10011).

National Association of Gay Alcoholism Professionals. *NAGAP bibliography: Resources on alcoholism and lesbians/gay men.* Spring 1981 (Revised ed.). (Available from NAGAP).

INDEX

Advocate Experience 54
Al-Anon 37,40,41,102
Alcohol Forum of the National Council on
    Alcoholism 102
Alcohol Treatment Unit, VAMC 29,31
    See also Veterans Administration Medical
    Center
Alcoholics Anonymous (AA) 4,11,37,44,47,
    49-50,58,64,65,66,67,102
    See also Gay AA
Alcoholism Center for Women in Los
    Angeles 11
alcoholism treatment, gays' fear of 48
alternative support system, in alcohol abuse
    prevention 93
anger work, use in therapy 58
Antabuse™ 17
    See also Disulfiram
assertiveness training 54
aversion techniques, as treatment 17
awareness therapy 61

bars
    See gay bar
baths (gay bath houses) 47,54,55
Beth' Achava, a Jewish gay organization 47
"bifocal approach" to therapy 53-54,56-57
biological intolerance to alcohol, theory of
    13-14
Boston Gay Health Collective 72

"casual" sex 60-61
causes of alcoholism and/or homosexuality
    3,10,13ff
Center for Multicultural Awareness 92
co-addiction 37ff
"coming out process," use of alcohol during
    19,21-22,34,49,64
compartmentalization of personality states
    59,62
compulsive sex 60,63

consciousness-raising activities 54,87
couples 3,47,64ff
couples, blame of partner 41
couples counseling 47-48
couples, fear of losing partner 40
cruising 47
cult-like orthodoxy, in AA meetings 86

denial of affectional differences, in AA
    meetings 82-83
denial system of alcoholics 49
Dignity, a Catholic gay organization 47
disclosure of sexual orientation 29-30
disease concepts of homosexuality 16,44
Disulfiram 46
    See also Antabuse™
double lives, therapy for 63-64
drinking patterns 11-12,17-19,72-73

ego reduction, used by AA 82
electric shock treatment 17
Erikson, Erik 67
est 54

family relations 20,22,38,39,49(footnote),
    65,71
    See also parents, couples

Gay AA 45,47,50,87,90,102
    See also Alcoholics Anonymous
gay bar 5,18,21,34,35,47,54,55,56,86
    (footnote)
Gay Caucus of the National Association of
    Alcoholism Counselors 103
Gay Community Services Center 11
Gay Health Collective 80
Gay Hotline 74
gay life-style, influence on alcohol use 18-19,
    21-22
Gay, Proud, and Sober (documentary film) 31
Gay Rights National Lobby 47

gay sponsor in AA meeting 87
genetic transmission of alcoholism 13-14
"getting high," a state of consciousness 61-62
group counseling 12,29-30,40,54,58
guilt concerning past sexual activity 62-63

Hazelden Educational Services 11
"high risk" individual, characteristics of 93
Homophile Alcoholism Treatment Service
    (HATS) 71-80
Homophile Community Health Services 71
homophobia 31,87

impotence 39,59,66,85
intervention, by co-alcoholics 37
intervention program, early 94-98

job interviews, problems with 49
Journal of Studies on Alcohol 9

latent homosexuality 10,14
latent homosexuality, and alcoholism 10,14-17
learned behavior, alcoholism as a 17-19
Lesbian Caucus of the Women in Crisis
    Conference 103

Massachusetts Rehabilitation Commission 74
Michigan Alcoholism Screening Test (MAST)
    12 ·
morbid dependency, of older gay alcoholic 67

National Association of Gay Alcoholism
    Professionals 11,101-103
National Council on Alcoholism 103
National Council on Alcoholism in Seattle 11
National Gay Health Coalition 103
National Gay Task Force 47,103
National Institute on Alcohol Abuse and
    Alcoholism 103
National Institute on Drug Abuse 92
Neo-Reichian body work 61

older gay male alcoholics 66

paranoia, in gay males 54
parents, alcoholic 13,38
partners
    See couples
pessimism, in older gay alcoholics 66-67
President's Commission on Mental Health 3,91
prevalence of alcoholism 5,9,11,27,34,35,
    72,81

prevention/early intervention program 89
problems related to alcoholism 27,49
psychoanalytic theories explaining alcoholism
    14,16
Public Health Service 89

rage 20
rate of alcoholism
    See prevalence
relationships
    See couples
religion, in AA meetings 85-86
Richmond, Mary 43
Rutgers Summer School on Alcohol Studies
    102

sadomasochism 65
second rate relationship labelling 64-65
self-enhancement strategies, in therapy 94-95
self-esteem, lowered, problems with 21-22,
    32,54,57-59,65,66,91
self-pleasuring exercises, use in treatment
    59-60
self-oppression 49
sex and intoxication 15,39,47,56,59,61
sexual compulsiveness 60-61
sexual dysfunction 39
    See also impotence
sexual orientation, disclosure of 29-30
sexual preference, denial of, in AA meetings
    83
sexual problems of gay alcoholic 59
sexual puritanism, in AA meetings 84-85
sex when sober, problems with 59
social bonding patterns 65-66
social sanctions, importance in explaining
    alcoholism 17-23,54
social values, divergence 4
    See also staff attitudes
sociological view of alcoholism 90
staff attitudes 4,28,32,50
staff training 29ff,34,50,71
stigma 5,20,22,44,49,54
Sullivan, Harry Stack 6
symptom prescription, use in therapy 58

Tantra practices 61
teenage alcoholism 6
therapy, limits and adverse effects 28,72,79,81
treatment center, support by gay community
    30-31,89-99

unconscious denial process, of alcoholics 22
  See also denial system
University of California at Irvine 102

Valley Forge Medical Center and Hospital 45
venereal disease, efforts to control 89

Veterans Administration Medical Center
  (VAMC) 29

Whitman-Walker Clinic's Gay Counsel on
  Drinking Behavior 90
Wisconsin Clearinghouse for Alcohol and
  Other Drug Information 11